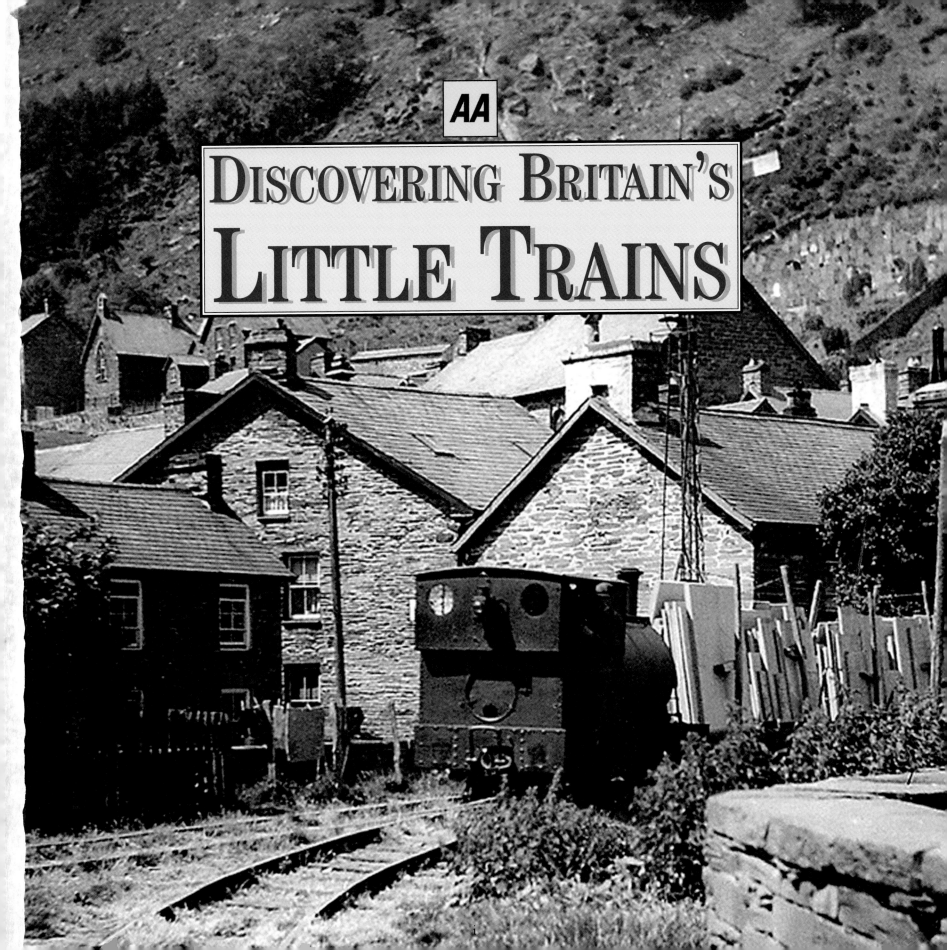

Discovering Britain's Little Trains

AA

DISCOVERING BRITAIN'S LITTLE TRAINS

JULIAN HOLLAND

Published by AA Publishing, a trading name of
Automobile Association Developments Limited, whose
registered office is Fanum House, Basing View,
Basingstoke, Hampshire RG21 4EA. Registered
Number 1878835.

Conceived and written by Julian Holland

A CIP catalogue record for this book is available from
the British Library.

A03757

Trade ISBN 978 07495 58673
Special Sales ISBN 978 07495 58895
Colour origination by Keenes Group, Andover.
Printed in China by C & C Offset Printing Co., Ltd

The contents of this book are believed correct at the
time of printing. Nevertheless, the Publishers cannot
accept responsibility for errors or omissions, or for
changes in details given.

Visit the AA Publishing website www.theAA.com/travel

CONTENTS

INTRODUCTION

*D*iscovering Britain's Little Trains takes the reader on a trip down memory lane to the eccentric world of Britain's narrow gauge railways. Many, such as the Ashover Light Railway in Derbyshire and the Welsh Highland Railway, were short lived and never lived up to the over-optimistic expectations of their promoters. Most of them had closed and had long disappeared into the undergrowth well before the onset of World War II.

While several preserved narrow gauge lines in Britain, such as the Ffestiniog Railway and Talyllyn Railway, are well-known to the public the author has chosen ten of the more idiosyncratic and less well-known lines to delight the reader. Armed with his trusty camera and with the resourcefulness of a 'railway detective', Julian Holland has unearthed some real gems that have lain hidden away - some for over 70 years - in Britain's countryside.

However, due to the dedicated efforts of preservationists, some are now in the process of being reopened. Julian Holland's fascinating text is accompanied by nostalgic photographs and ephemera of both closed and reopened lines in their heyday, along with specially commissioned colour photographs of what can be seen today.

Right *Hidden away in a remote valley in the scenic Peak District, the Leek & Manifold Valley Light Railway had a very short life of only 30 years. Following closure in 1934, the trackbed, including Swainsley Tunnel, seen on the right, was given by its owners, the London Midland & Scottish Railway, to Staffordshire County Council to use as a footpath and cycleway.*

Other photos: Half-title page: *A slate train trundles through Corris shortly before closure of the Corris Railway.* Title page: *Douglas Station on the Isle of Man Railway.* Contents page: *A passenger train for Chirk gets ready to leave Glyn Ceiriog on the Glyn Valley Tramway in August 1926.*

WHERE TO FIND THE LITTLE TRAINS

Campbeltown & Machrihanish Light Railway
132–141

Isle of Man Railways
142–155

Glyn Valley Tramway
84–99

Ashover Light Railway
56–69

Welsh Highland Railway
100–115

Corris Railway
116–131

Leek & Manifold Valley Light Railway
70–83

Southwold Railway
42–55

Lynton & Barnstaple Railway
8–27

Rye & Camber Tramway
28–41

LYNTON & BARNSTAPLE RAILWAY

BARNSTAPLE TOWN TO LYNTON

With a population of around 35,000, Barnstaple is by far the largest town in North Devon and is possibly one of the oldest boroughs in the United Kingdom. Located at the lowest crossing point on the River Taw, a settlement probably existed here even before the Roman occupation and, by Norman times, Barnstaple was important enough to have its own mint. During the Middle Ages, the town was an important merchant and naval port exporting large quantities of wool and, later, supplying ships to fight against the Spanish Armada. To this day, farming has always played an important role in the local economy of Barnstaple and the surrounding area.

By contrast, the village of Lynton together with its lower neighbour Lynmouth, on the North Devon coast, owes much of its development to the Victorian politician and publisher Sir George Newnes, who built a mansion for himself on Hollerday Hill above the village. Newnes not only built the famous Lynton & Lynmouth Cliff Railway but also provided the Town Hall and Congregational Church. Notably, he was also instrumental in the building of the Lynton & Barnstaple Railway in his bid to promote tourism in this area.

Today, the local economy of this beautiful part of North Devon is still heavily dependent on both farming and tourism.

Railways first came to North Devon in 1848 with the opening of a horse drawn tramway between Barnstaple and Fremington Quay. By 1854, the North Devon Railway (later to become part of the London & South Western Railway) had opened its line from Exeter to Barnstaple where the station was named Barnstaple Junction. The Fremington line became steam hauled and was extended west to Bideford and later to Torrington.

Meanwhile, the Great Western Railway had its sights on reaching Barnstaple and Ilfracombe. In 1873, the company opened its line from Taunton to Barnstaple (Victoria Road) via Dulverton. The following year the London & South Western Railway opened its line from Barnstaple Junction to Ilfracombe, via a new bridge over the River Taw. A new station, Barnstaple Quay but later renamed Barnstaple Town, was also opened on the opposite side of the river.

The final piece of the Barnstaple standard gauge jigsaw was put into place in 1885 when the GWR opened its link between Victoria Road Station and Junction Station. Through running between Taunton (and beyond) and Ilfracombe was now possible.

Below *Introduced in 1923 by the Southern Railway Manning, Wardle 2-6-2 tank No. 188* Lew *is seen here at Pilton in May 1935. Four months later the line closed and* Lew *was eventually shipped off to Brazil, never to be seen again!*

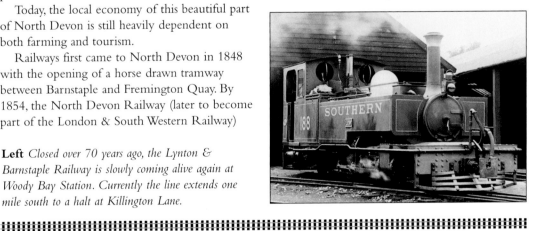

Left *Closed over 70 years ago, the Lynton & Barnstaple Railway is slowly coming alive again at Woody Bay Station. Currently the line extends one mile south to a halt at Killington Lane.*

HISTORY OF THE RAILWAY

By the mid-19th century the twin villages of Lynton and Lynmouth, known as 'the little Switzerland of England', were fast becoming popular as a holiday destination for the middle-classes. The opening of the standard gauge railways to Barnstaple improved communications and brought more visitors to the area. Those trying to reach Lynton, however, were then faced with a lengthy horsedrawn coach journey of nearly three hours on the steeply graded packhorse road over Exmoor. There now grew a demand for a railway to be built to Lynton and several proposals, including an electrified line, were put forward. None of these saw the light of day, due mainly to high construction costs that would have been needed to build a standard gauge railway in such difficult terrain.

Meanwhile, in North Wales, the building of narrow gauge railways through difficult terrain

Below *Charles Drewett, General Manager of the Lynton & Barnstaple Railway from 1899 to 1923, was responsible for the issue of several series of official postcards depicting views of the railway in the early 20th century.*

Right *Barnstaple Town Station opened in 1874 with the completion of the L&SWR line to Ilfracombe. It was later joined by the Lynton & Barnstaple Railway in 1895. The station closed in 1970 and is now a school.*

had already proved to be a success. In particular, the 1ft 11½in gauge Ffestiniog Railway showed that construction costs could be much reduced because of the line's ability to follow the contours of the land, by using much sharper curves than the standard gauge. Back in Lynton a group of local wealthy businessmen, including the publisher Sir George Newnes, put forward a proposal to build a narrow gauge line from Barnstaple Town station with estimated construction costs of £2,500 per mile. Backed by Sir George, this scheme soon found favour with the local populace and a petition to the House of Commons for the Lynton & Barnstaple Railway Bill was approved at a meeting in May 1895.

The Lynton & Barnstaple Railway Bill received Royal Assent in June 1895 and Sir James Szlumper was appointed Consultant Engineer of the 19-mile line. Amidst great

Lynton and Barnstaple Railway. Barnstaple Town Station.

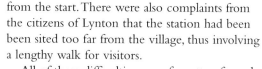

from the start. There were also complaints from the citizens of Lynton that the station had been been sited too far from the village, thus involving a lengthy walk for visitors.

All of these difficulties were forgotten for a day when the railway was opened on 11 May 1898 by Sir George and Lady Newnes. Large crowds turned out all along the line to cheer on the flag-bedecked train.

Above *One of the first photographs ever taken by railway photographer Ivo Peters when he was only 10-years-old. Exe waits at the head of a mixed train at Barnstaple Town in August 1925 only two years after takeover of the railway by the Southern Railway.*

Below *Located ½-mile from Barnstaple Town, the yard at Pilton was the headquarters of the Lynton & Barnstaple Railway and contained locomotive and carriage sheds, Manager's office, goods yard, turntable and repair shops. After closure the site became a timber yard but the buildings were destroyed in a fire in 1992.*

celebrations the first sod was cut by Lady Newnes in September. Nothing ever goes to plan, however, and the building of the Lynton & Barnstaple was no exception. Work began in March 1896 but difficulties soon arose during excavation for the trackbed due to unforeseen rock, and necessary blasting, that was encountered. Purchase of the land for the railway also proved to be much more expensive than estimated. Including expensive litigation, the extra costs incurred doubled the original estimate for the building of the railway, financially crippling it

To run the railway, the company had purchased three brand new 2-6-2 tank locomotives from Manning, Wardle & Co of Leeds. Of a very handsome design, they were given the names of local rivers -*Yeo*, *Exe* and *Taw*. Within a short time it became necessary to purchase a fourth locomotive and an order was placed with the Baldwin Locomotive Works in Philadelphia for a 2-4-2 tank which, on delivery, was named *Lyn*.

To cope with the large numbers of passengers that the company had forecast would use the new line, the passenger coaching stock ordered was on a grand scale. All but one of the 17 35ft bogie coaches, including a 1st Class observation car, were built by the Bristol Wagon & Carriage Company. Large amounts of coal were also expected to be transported on the new line from a new quay on the River Yeo at Barnstaple. To

cope with this and more general goods traffic, the company ordered over 20 goods wagons, many of them also carried on bogies.

Below *The majority of the trackbed of the Lynton & Barnstaple Railway is now on private property. Nestling in the picturesque valley of the River Yeo, this road overbridge still stands over the long-closed line between Snapper Halt and Chelfham*

Built to a very high standard, the line was fully signalled and three of the nine stations, Blackmoor, Woody Bay and Lynton, were built in a very pleasing style reminiscent of Swiss chalets. By far the most impressive feat of narrow gauge engineering in Britain was the 70ft-high Chelfham Viaduct that took the Lynton & Barnstaple across the Stoke Rivers valley on eight arches. Built entirely of Marland bricks, it still stands majestically today awaiting the reopening of the line.

From the start there were many complaints from passengers about the service on the line. Most of the trains were of the mixed variety and included passenger carriages and goods wagons in their makeup, and the journey often overran the 1hr 50min allowed in the timetable due to shunting at intermediate stations. There were also complaints about the unnerving rolling of the carriages and of the distance of Lynton station from the village.

The timetable allowed for five trains a day each way on Modays to Saturdays. A single train each way sufficed for Sundays. Passenger numbers steadily increased from around 76,000 in 1901 to a peak of 109,000 in 1913. Passenger traffic was very heavy during the summer with many holidaymakers transferring from main line trains at Barnstaple Town before the last leg of their journey to Lynton. The picture was rather different during the winter, although freight remained fairly constant throughout the year. The mainstay of freight receipts came from coal which was transhipped from coasters at Pilton Wharf and taken by train to various stations along the line. However, the majority of this traffic was always destined for Lynton where it was distributed by a local coal merchant from his horse and cart.

The Ilfracombe to Lynton road journey had for years been handled by horsedrawn coaches and then by motor buses. Heavily used during the

Left *Chelfham Viaduct is by far the most impressive engineering work on the Lynton & Barnstaple Railway. Recently restored, the 8-arch viaduct, built of local white Marland bricks, towers 70ft above the Yeo Valley and is the largest narrow gauge structure in Britain. Costing £6,500 to build, it patiently awaits the reopening of the railway.*

Right *One of the beautiful series of coloured postcards produced by the Lynton & Barnstaple Railway in the early 20th century. This one depicts Chelfham Viaduct shortly after opening. Today the view of the viaduct from the valley floor is partly obscured by trees.*

Below *Manning, Wardle 2-6-2 tank Lew arriving at Chelfham. The Lynton & Barnstaple Railway was taken over in 1923 by the Southern Railway who set about relaying track, refurbishing carriages, installing new fencing and modernising signalling. Lew was delivered in 1925 and worked the final tracklifting trains in 1936. She was sold at auction and shipped off to Brazil - never to be seen again!*

Lynton and Barnstaple Railway. Chelfham Station and Viaduct.

Major, Darker & Lorraine (Photo).

SOUTHERN 759

summer, this was a lucrative market that the Lynton & Barnstaple intended to capture. In 1903 Sir George Newnes set about buying two motor coaches which would run from Ilfracombe to Blackmoor station where they would connect with a train for Lynton.

This first experiment by any railway to run a motor coach feeder service was shortlived due to the bus drivers being fined for speeding by the

Below *After 70 years of closure, this low embankment and Southern Railway concrete fence posts are clearly visible from the unclassified road that runs between Chelfham and Bratton Cross.*

local police! The coaches were subsequently sold to the GWR, who used them on their Helston to Lizard route.

The driving force behind the development of Lynton into a tourist resort and the building of the Lynton & Barnstaple Railway, Sir George Newnes, died in 1910. He was replaced as Chairman of the railway by Sir Thomas Hewitt, who was immediately faced with the growing problem of competition from road transport. However, the little railway soldiered on through World War I until 1922, when the impact from the competition really started to bite. The

financial situation for the company was now dire and it was only saved by the Railway Grouping of 1923 when the newly formed Southern Railway took control.

The Southern Railway immediately set about modernising the rundown Lynton & Barnstaple. Track was relaid, new fencing was erected, improvements were made to signalling, passenger carriages were refurbished, new goods wagons built and a new Manning, Wardle 2-6-2 tank locomotive was ordered. On delivery it was named *Lew*. Sadly, none of this investment made any difference to the railway's fortunes. Major

road improvements in the area led to a continuing increase in competition from motor coaches and cars and, although the line was still heavily used by holidaymakers during the summer, the writing was now on the wall for the little railway. Consequently the Southern Railway decided to close the line on 29 September 1935.

Right *Another of the beautiful series of coloured postcards issued by the Lynton & Barnstaple Railway in the early 20th century. Here, Taw, its train, crew and passengers pose on a low embankment for the local photographer.*

Lynton and Barnstaple Railway.

Major, Darker & Lorraine (Photo).

Major, Darker & Lorraine (Photo).

Lynton and Barnstaple Railway. Bratton Fleming Station.

On that sad day the last heavily-loaded train, double-headed by *Lew* and *Yeo*, pulled out of Lynton Station for the final time. In the driving rain and gathering gloom, the train ended its journey at Barnstaple Town where it was met by hundreds of onlookers. After only 37 years of faithful service to this beautiful part of North Devon, the Lynton & Barnstaple Railway was no more. Rolling stock and locomotives were all collected at Pilton yard to await sale by auction, which was held in November 1935. Appallingly, all of the locomotives apart from *Lew* were sold for scrap for about £50 each and

Left *Bratton Fleming station beautifully depicted in this official postcard issued by the Lynton & Barnstaple Railway soon after opening. The station building is now a private residence.*

Above *The trackbed of the Lynton & Barnstaple Railway at Hunnacott, north of Bratton Fleming. Half a mile to the north the trackbed was flooded in 1956 by the construction of Wistlandpound Reservoir.*

many of the passenger carriages ended their days as garden huts or sheds. After assisting in track lifting operations in May 1936, *Lew* was shipped off to Brazil - never to be seen again! Stations and trackbed were sold off piecemeal in October 1938. Sadly missed by many holidaymakers, the Lynton & Barnstaple Railway had come to the end of the line - or had it? On closure a wreath had been laid on the buffer stop at Barnstaple Town - it read: *Perchance it's not dead but sleepeth.*

Right *Heading south towards Bratton Fleming, the trackbed of the railway passes under this arched overbridge near Narracott. In a few years time this idyllic spot could well witness the return of steam trains.*

Lynton and Barnstaple Railway. Blackmoor Gate Station.

THE LINE TODAY

Over 70 years since it closed, much of the route of the Lynton & Barnstaple Railway can still be traced today. Although most of the trackbed itself is now on private property, it is fairly easy to follow it from adjacent roads and lanes.

The standard gauge line from Barnstaple to Ilfracombe closed in 1970, but Barnstaple Town station has been preserved and is now in use as a school. Unfortunately, the L&B sheds and works at Pilton have been destroyed by fire, but the route of the line can be rejoined by driving from Barnstaple through Waytown to the site of Snapper Halt in the lush Yeo Valley. From here lanes parallel the trackbed through Chelfham and Bratton Fleming as far as Hunnacott, just south of the Wistlandpound Reservoir. The major engineering work on the Lynton & Barnstaple, the graceful Chelfham Viaduct, still stands today

Left *Blackmoor station is now a restaurant called the 'Old Railway Inn'. Remains of the L&B can be found in its grounds, including the base of the water tower (now a shed) and an SR concrete signal post.*

Above *Depicted in an official postcard just after opening, Blackmoor station clearly shows the attractive Swiss chalet style of architecture adopted during the building of the railway.*

and has recently been restored with new parapets in readiness for the possible reopening of the line.

Set in woodland high above the Yeo Valley, the Chelfham station site, including the station bungalow, former station master's house and trackbed were purchased in 1998 by a consortium consisting of the Lynton & Barnstaple Railway Association (founded in 1979) and individual members. The station master's house, Distant Point, has been restored and is used by members as a holiday home.

Bratton Fleming station building is now a private residence and the trackbed of the railway between Narracott, where there is a well preserved arched railway bridge, and Sprecott has been converted into a road. However, keen eyes will spot the regulation Southern Railway

Lynton and Barnstaple Railway. Woody Bay Station.

concrete fence posts that were erected in 1923. North of Sprecott a section of the L&B trackbed has been flooded by the construction of Wistlandpound Reservoir which was completed in 1956. The formation of the railway can still be seen when water levels are low.

To the north of the reservoir, Blackmoor station is now a pub and restaurant called the 'Old Railway Inn', with remains of the L&B water tank and a concrete signal post set in landscaped grounds. Never far from the busy A39, the line winds its way up Parracombe Bank to Churchtown where the road overbridge has been underfilled and a modern bungalow has been built over the trackbed. Another mile takes us to the Lynton & Barnstaple Railway's rebirth - Woody Bay station. Located nearly 1,000ft above sea level and 1½ miles from the coast, there are

Left *Recently reopened by the Lynton & Barnstaple Railway Association, the stretch of track between Woody Bay and Killington Lane offers panoramic views of the North Devon countryside from its vantage point 900ft above sea level.*

Above *Official L&B postcard of Woody Bay Station shortly after opening. Today, the trackbed beyond the platform is the location of the Lynton & Barnstaple Railway Association's locomotive and carriage sheds.*

fine views toward the sea from here.

Purchased by the Lynton & Barnstaple Railway Association in 1995, Woody Bay station has been totally restored, a locomotive and carriage shed has been erected and a section of track has been relaid for a distance of a mile south to a temporary station and run-round loop at Killington Lane. Several original L&B coaches and items of goods rolling stock, once used as sheds or summer houses, are being restored by members and it is hoped one day to build a replica Manning, Wardle tank locomotive. The long term aim of the Society is to reopen the entire railway and, with this in mind, parcels of land along the route are currently being purchased. Steam and diesel hauled passenger trains operate on most weekends throughout the year from Woody Bay with a more intensive daily

Above *Works plate on newly restored Van No. 23, which is currently without steel frame or bogies and is being used to house an exhibition of the line at Woody Bay station. The 8-ton brake van was rescued in a sorry state from a field in North Devon.*

Left *Viewed from the driver's cab of the line's resident diesel, a train from Killington Lane approaches the beautifully restored Woody Bay station. The railway's locomotive and carriage shed can be seen in the cutting beyond the station.*

Below *The Lynton & Barnstaple Railway passed through some of the most beautiful scenery in Britain. These far-reaching views towards Exmoor were a regular sight from the train as it approached Caffyn's Halt.*

Above *The penultimate stop before Lynton, Caffyn's Halt was opened in 1907 to serve a local golf course. It was not a popular place for southbound trains to stop as it was located on a 1 in 50 gradient.*

Above *24 May 1935 - only four months before closure of the Lynton & Barnstaple Railway - Manning, Wardle 2-6-2 tank Yeo waits at Lynton station with a four coach train for Barnstaple.*

Left *Due to its distance from the village, the siting of Lynton station - 700ft above sea level and 250ft above Lynton - was always a bone of contention with locals. With its Swiss chalet style much in evidence, the well preserved building is now a private residence.*

service from April to October. For more information on the Society and details of train running times contact the Lynton & Barnstaple Railway Association, Woody Bay Station, Martinhoe Cross, Parracombe, Devon EX31 4RA (tel. 01598 763487) or visit the Society's website: www.lynton-rail.co.uk

Continuing on from Woody Bay, the trackbed of the railway is clearly visible to the right of the A39 near the site of Caffyn's Halt. The halt was opened in 1907 to serve a local golf course and was not a popular place for southbound trains to stop as it was located on a 1 in 50 gradient.

We finally reach the end of the line at Lynton station, which remains in fairly original condition as a private house. The adjoining goods shed has been converted into holiday homes. Perhaps one day in the future steam trains will once more arrive here after conveying holidaymakers along one of Britain's most scenic railways.

SIR GEORGE NEWNES

Sir George Newnes, born in Matlock, Derbyshire in 1851, went on to become one of the most successful magazine publishers in London. During the latter part of the 19th century, he founded many well known magazine titles including Tit-Bits, Country Life and The Strand Magazine - famous for its publication of Sir Arthur Conan Doyle's stories of Sherlock Holmes.

In addition to running his publishing empire, Newnes was also MP for Newmarket between 1885 and 1895.

Newnes moved to North Devon in 1892 and built a mansion near Lynton. He became a great benefactor of the village by building the Lynton & Lynmouth Cliff Railway, Lynton Town Hall and Congregational Church. He was also one of the driving forces behind the building of the Lynton & Barnstaple Railway of which was Chairman until his death in 1910.

Right *A beautifully coloured official railway postcard showing Lynton station soon after opening.*

ORDNANCE SURVEY MAP
Landranger 1:50,000 series No.180

TOURIST INFORMATION
Barnstaple: Barnstaple Tourist Information Centre, The Square, Barnstaple, Devon EX32 8LN (tel. 01271 375000) or visit: www.staynorthdevon.co.uk
Lynton: Lynton & Lynmouth Tourist Information Centre, Town Hall, Lee Road, Lynton, Devon EX35 6BT (tel. 0845 6603232) or visit: www.lynton-lynmouth-tourism.co.uk

WHERE TO STAY
There is a wide range of accommodation in this area of North Devon. For more details contact either Barnstaple or Lynton Tourist Information Centres (see above).

RAILWAY WALKS
As the majority of the Lynton & Barnstaple trackbed is currently on privately owned land, walkers should avoid trespassing. However, it is still possible to walk along part of the line that is now a public road between Narracott, north of Bratton Fleming, to Sprecott. From here a footpath follows the line as far as Wistlandpound Reservoir, ½ mile south of Blackmoor Gate.

PLACES TO VISIT
● Tarka Trail
● Barnstaple Pannier Market
● Marwood Hill Gardens
● Broomhill Sculpture Garden
● Museum of North Devon, Barnstaple
● Arlington Court (NT)
● Heddon Hill Gardens, Parracombe
● Exmoor Zoological Park, Bratton Fleming
● Lynbarn Railway, nr Clovelly
● Lynton & Lynmouth Cliff Railway
● Lyn & Exmoor Museum, Lynton
● Watersmeet (NT)

Lynton and Barnstaple Railway. Lynton and Lynmouth Station.

RYE & CAMBER TRAMWAY

RYE TO CAMBER SANDS

The historic hilltop town of Rye in East Sussex is located on the western edge of part of Romney Marsh known as Walland Marsh. Rye received its town charter during Norman times. Due to its stategically important location, the town was fortified by King Stephen, who also established a mint here in the twelfth century. One of Rye's ancient gateways, Landgate, and Ypres Tower still survive today.

Now almost two miles inland, Rye was once an important port and became one of the two ancient towns that supported the Confederation of Cinque Ports, which was formed in 1155 to provide ships and defences in support of the defence of the realm. However, due to severe weather conditions during the latter half of the 13th century, the sea broke through the coastal shingle banks and flooded large areas of land along the coastline. Violent storms, in particular those of 1287, caused a further build up of shingle extending the coastline up to two miles further out to sea, and Rye's importance as a port was severely diminished. Much of the surrounding marshland formed by this flooding had been reclaimed and drained by the 16th century.

Rye's importance in the defence of the realm came to the fore again in the 16th century when Henry VIII built Camber Castle to protect the town from threatened invasion by France. During the Napoleonic Wars of the early 19th century, a string of 74 Martello Towers were built at strategic locations along this part of the south coast between Folkestone and Seaford. A fine example of one of these defensive towers can be seen today at Rye Harbour.

As a further line of defence against French invasion, the Royal Military Canal was built following the course of the former coastline that formed the boundary of Romney Marsh. Construction of the 28-mile canal started in 1804 and was completed in 1809. The canal, which was fortified with pillboxes during World War II and is now an important environmental site with several Sites of Special Scientific Interest, flows around the town of Rye. A public footpath follows the whole route of the canal.

Just over two miles to the southeast of Rye, Camber Sands is the only sand dune system in East Sussex and is designated a Site of Special Scientific Interest.

Left *An attractive young lady poses on the deserted and weed-infested platform of Golf Links Halt on 12 July 1931. By that date, the eccentric Rye & Camber Tramway was in terminal decline.*

Above *Built by W G Bagnall of Stafford, diminutive 2-4-0 tank locomotive Camber, here seen at Rye in 1931, was the first locomotive to operate trains on the Rye & Camber Tramway when it opened in 1895.*

Camber-on-Sea' painted in large white letters on the Rye side of the building. A corrugated iron shed was also built to accommodate the tramway's motive power and rolling stock. The corrugated iron building of the original Camber terminus, later named Golf Links Halt after the line was extended in 1908, bore a similar resemblance in style to Rye station. With an intermediate request stop at Halfway House (later known as Squatter's Right), the 1¾ mile line was officially opened on 13 July 1895 by the Mayoress of Rye. Services were provided by one passenger coach and two open wagons hauled by a small 2-4-0 steam tank locomotive, *Camber*, which had been built by W. G. Bagnall of Stafford.

Above *With the historic hilltop town of Rye in the background, the former trackbed of the Rye & Camber disappears into the distance before terminating at the site of the Rye terminus adjacent to Monkbretton Bridge.*

HISTORY OF THE RAILWAY

Railways first came to Rye in 1851 when the South Eastern Railway opened a 26-mile line between Hastings and Ashford. The line, now known as the Marshlink Line, fortunately not only escaped the Beeching closures of the 1960s but also more recent threats, provides a very useful service to this historic town. A short freight branch line to Rye Harbour was opened in 1854 and closed in 1962.

Rapid expansion of the railways, consequent ease of mass transport and growth in leisure time, saw Victorian Britain experiencing major social changes in the late 19th century. The game of golf was also increasing in popularity and that is why the Rye & Camber Tramway was conceived.

At that time no golf club existed at Rye or Hastings and the nearest, at Littlestone, would not take on any new members. Certain leading lights in Rye therefore proposed the opening of a local club and a suitable site was found among the sand dunes of Camber Sands. Rye Golf Club officially opened in February 1894 but there still existed

the problem of transport from the town to Camber Sands. Although the Monkbretton road bridge across the River Rother was opened in 1895, the road to the golf club was little more than a muddy track and golfers would arrive back in Rye after their game in a very wretched state.

To overcome this lack of transport various local businessmen proposed the building of a tramway from Monkbretton Bridge to Rye Golf Club. As it was planned to build the line on private land no Act of Parliament was required for the construction of the line. The Rye & Camber Tramways Company Ltd came into being in April 1895 and construction of the 3ft narrow gauge line was overseen by Colonel H. F Stephens who was soon to become famous for running an idiosyncratic railway empire from his headquarters in Tonbridge.

Initially the lightly laid line ran from a terminus adjacent to Monkbretton Bridge on the eastern outskirts of Rye to Camber Station opposite Rye Harbour. The station at Rye bore a great resemblance in style to Colonel H F Stephens' stations that he had built on his first line, the Cranbrook & Paddock Wood Railway which had opened in 1892. Built of corrugated iron it was livened up with decorative barge boards and later had the lettering 'Tram to

The little line was an immediate hit with golfers, fishermen and local day trippers, with around 18,000 passengers using it in the first six months of operation. Buoyed by this success the company ordered a second passenger coach which was delivered in 1896, and a second 2-4-0 tank locomotive, *Victoria*, which was delivered by Bagnalls in 1897.

Despite a few lean years, particularly during the winter months when the line was subsidised by Rye Golf Club and the local Mayor, the company made a decision in 1906 to extend the line to a new terminus in the sand dunes near Camber Sands. The latter station simply consisted of a wooden platform made from old railway sleepers, and with no shelter for waiting passengers. The extension, built almost entirely on an embankment close to the golf links, was opened on 13 July 1908 and the original terminus was renamed Golf Links Halt. Advertised in the tramway's timetable as 'far from the madding crowd' and an invigorating health resort, Camber Sands soon became a popular spot for day trippers and picnickers in the summer months. Hidden away in the sand dunes over half a mile from Camber, the sparse station was joined at a later date by a small tea room. Little freight was carried on the line apart from sand, which was carried to Rye for sale to local builders. Despite good passenger receipts during the summer months when up to 15 trains each way were run, the line still struggled to survive during the winter months and became dependent on subsidies from Rye Golf Club until 1924.

Below *Typical of the corrugated iron stations so beloved by the line's engineer, WH Stephens, Rye terminus slumbers on during a sunny day in April 1931. In the foreground is the engine and carriage shed.*

Left *The Rye & Camber 3ft gauge, forever preserved in concrete near the site of Squatter's Right. From here to the Broadwater stream, the route of the tramway has disappeared beneath a more recently formed lake.*

Along with other British narrow gauge lines, however, by the mid-1920s the Rye & Camber Tramway began to see its fortunes decline. Competition from road transport, coupled with the high cost of coal and repairs to the two steam locomotives, forced the company to look at cheaper forms of motive power. In 1925, a small petrol rail tractor was purchased and was found to be ideally suited to hauling most of the trains on the line. *Victoria* was soon scrapped and *Camber* spent most of its time out of use in the shed at Rye. Furthermore, with the ending of the subsidy from the golf club, all winter services were suspended for good in 1926. The tramway struggled on into the 1930s and still gave great pleasure to those day trippers who continued to use it in the summer months. Already struggling financially, the end came for the Rye & Camber

Tramway as a passenger-carrying enterprise with the outbreak of World War II in 1939. Even without the war, it is debatable whether the line could have continued to operate for much longer. If it had managed to struggle through to the 1950s, it might just have been saved by the pioneering railway preservationists of that time.

However, this was not quite the end of the line for the Rye & Camber Tramway. During World War II, the section of line between Rye and Golf Links Halt was requisitioned by the Admiralty. Men and materials were conveyed on the line to support the building of a large jetty on the Camber side of Rye Harbour. Road access from the Rye to Camber road was also improved to the construction site by concreting either side of the tramway's rails between Squatter's Right and Golf Links Halt. The well-preserved concreted rails can still be seen today along this stretch of the line and at Golf Links Halt. At the end of the war, the tramway was handed back to its owners

by the Admiralty in a very rundown state and was never reopened. The Rye & Camber Tramway Company was finally wound up in 1947 and steam locomotive *Camber* and the petrol tractor were sold for scrap. The final end of this unique and eccentric English railway went virtually unnoticed locally.

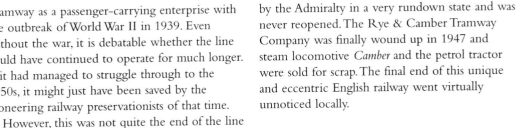

Below *Another view of the delectable young lady waiting at Golf Links Halt in July 1931. By this date the original loop line here had been lifted and the tramway was in decline. The section of line from here to Rye was taken over by the Admiralty in World War II.*

Right *Although the platform has long gone and the front awning section has been filled in, the corrugated iron building of Golf Links Halt remains in remarkably good condition today.*

THE LINE TODAY

Despite its relatively short working life and having been closed for over 60 years, there is still a surprising amount to be seen today of the Rye & Camber Tramway. The terminus buildings at Rye have long since disappeared and have been replaced by a pumping station but the site, adjacent to Monkbretton Bridge on the eastern outskirts of Rye, is easily accessible. From here the route of the line is now a wide path parallelling the River Rother as far as the the Broadwater stream. The current footpath veers to the left here, but the site of the railway bridge can still be seen with its original abutments and girders now supporting a pipeline.

Beyond the Broadwater Bridge is Northpoint Beach, where there was once a shingle extraction works. This is now a large lake which has flooded the tramway route at this point. Beyond here the route can be easily traced along a concreted road that skirts Rye Golf Club and provides access from the Rye to Camber road to the harbourmaster's house and inshore rescue station opposite Rye Harbour. Formerly the

Above *Following requisition by the Admiralty in World War II the Rye & Camber track was infilled with concrete to allow road access to the construction site of a new jetty near Golf Links Halt. Today the reinstated loop line and part of a siding to Rother Pier still remain in situ.*

Right *By now rarely in steam, 2-4-0 tank Camber poses at Rye with the line's diminutive petrol tractor in April 1931. Both locomotives were sold for scrap in 1947 after the line's closure.*

RYE GOLF CLUB

At the end of the 19th century no golf club existed at Rye or Hastings and the nearest, at Littlestone, would not take on any new members. A meeting was held at the George Hotel in Rye in late 1893 and it was agreed that a golf club should be formed, with the links to be located in the Camber sand dunes. The course was quickly laid out and the first competition held in February 1894. Chairman of the Rye Golf Club committee was the Rev J L Bates and H S Colt, a solicitor, was elected as the Captain. Colt, who designed the 18-hole course of 1895, went on to become a famous golf course designer. A wooden clubhouse was also built in 1894 and it is still in use today. Transport to the golf club was provided by the Rye & Camber Tramway, which opened in 1895. The Club was an immediate success and, by the turn of the century, there were around 250 members, including many from London.

By 1911 there were over 500 members, and the wooden clubhouse had been expanded to its present size. Close links between the Rye Golf Club and the Oxford and Cambridge Golfing Society were established at the end of the 19th century, and they remain so today. First played in 1920 between the two clubs, the 'President's Putter' soon became the most important event in the Rye calendar. Until 1932, several holes were located on the wrong side of the Rye to Camber road. With increasing traffic, play became dangerous, and the same year saw a major redesign of the course. For more details of the Rye Golf Club visit: www.ryegolfclub.co.uk

route of the tramway, this stretch of private road contains long sections of 3ft gauge track, preserved for ever in the concrete that was added during World War II.

Surprisingly, Golf Links Halt station building remains in a very well preserved state. Although the platform has long gone and with the front awning section filled in, the corrugated iron building has stood the test of time for over 100 years. In front of the station much of the old railway track, complete with loop line and a truncated section of a short siding to Rother Pier, remains perfectly preserved in the concrete that was added by the Admiralty during the war.

From Golf Links Halt, the 1908 extension to Camber Sands can easily be followed along the footpath that runs along the top of the tramway's low embankment. Now cutting straight through the fairways of Rye Golf Club, walkers along this official footpath should always be aware of flying golf balls!

Right *With the railway's entire rolling stock filled to capacity, A Rye & Camber train poses for the photographer amongst the sand dunes near Camber Sands. Although this was a common sight during the summer months until the mid 1920s, the Rye & Camber struggled to survive during the lean winter months and was frequently bailed out with a subsidy from Rye Golf Club.*

Rye and Camber Tramway

Below *The well-defined embankment of the 1908 extension from Golf Links Halt to Camber Sands is now an official footpath that bisects Rye Golf Club.*

COLONEL H F STEPHENS

Holman Fred Stephens, the son of the pre-Raphaelite artist Frederic George Stephens, was born in 1868 and went on to become a leading exponent of the building and managing of light railways in England and Wales. After studying civil engineering, Stephens went on to enrol as an apprentice at the Neasden Works of the Metropolitan Railway in 1881. His first job was as assistant engineer during the construction of the Cranbrook & Paddock Wood Railway, which opened in 1892. In the anticipation of the 1896 Light Railways Act, Stephens set up a company called the Light Railway Syndicate. This was not particularly successful and only one of his proposals saw the light of day, with the opening of the Sheppey Light Railway in 1901.

Despite this initial failure, Stephens went on to become highly successful in the building and managing of light railways in his own right. His first, the 3ft-gauge Rye & Camber Tramway, was opened in 1895 and, because it was built on private land, preceded the Light Railways Act by one year. His first proper light railway, the Rother Valley (later extended and finally known as the Kent & East Sussex Railway), between Robertsbridge and Rolvenden in Kent, was opened in 1900. Between 1900 and his untimely death in 1931, Stephens ran his railway empire from an office in Tonbridge. Following his death, his second-in-command, William Henry Austen, took over the far-flung railway empire.

In addition to the three lines already mentioned, other lines that were built and managed by Stephens included the Hundred of Manhood & Selsey Tramway, Weston, Clevedon & Portishead Railway, Shropshire & Montgomeryshire Railway, and the East Kent Light Railway.

Below *In an effort to reduce running costs the Rye & Camber purchased a petrol locomotive from the Kent Construction Company in Ashford in 1925. It proved so successful that one of the line's steam locomotives, Victoria, was sold for scrap.*

Left *To the untrained eye the site of Camber Sands station has completely disappeared. However, on closer examination these ferns provide the clue to where the wooden platform once stood.*

Below *The 4-wheel Simplex petrol locomotiove and one of the line's two coaches stand at Camber Sands station in the early 1930s. The driver had to sit sideways in the tiny cramped cab of this totally functional machine.*

RYE AND CAMBER TRAM.

After dodging the golf balls, we finally arrive at the site of the Camber Sands terminus. To the untrained eye there is nothing left of this basic timber platform, and it is easy to walk past the site without knowing it. However, the exact position of the station is marked by the presence of ferns which have thrived on the rotting timber over the past 70 years since the extension closed.

It is easy to imagine how this tranquil location nestling in the sand dunes was once advertised by the Rye & Camber Tramway in its timetable as being 'far from the madding crowd'. Where day trippers from Rye once sat in the sunshine with their picnics, there are now only skylarks, golfers with their trolleys and locals walking their dogs.

In 1939, an extension to the tramway beyond the site of Camber Sands station had been completed, but was never used due to the outbreak of war and the subsequent closure of the line. Today just concrete fencing posts and the World War II concrete pilboxes remind us of the end of this delightful little railway.

Right *The sand dunes at Camber Sands were once described in the Rye & Camber Tramway's timetable as 'far from the madding crowd' and an invigorating health resort.*

Below *A group of small boys show a keen interest in the petrol locomotive at Camber Sands in April 1931. By this date the station not only boasted a simple wooden shelter but also an adjacent tea room.*

ORDNANCE SURVEY MAP
Landranger 1:50,000 series No. 189

TOURIST INFORMATION
Rye Tourist Information Centre, The Heritage Centre, Strand Quay, Rye, East Sussex TN31 7AY (tel: 01797 226696) or visit www.visitrye.co.uk

WHERE TO STAY
There is a wide range of accommodation in the Rye and Camber area. For more details contact Rye Tourist Information Centre (see above), or for details of accommodation in Camber visit: www.camber.east-sussex.co.uk

RAILWAY WALKS
Apart from the flooded section at Northpoint Beach, the entire 2½ mile route of the Rye & Camber tramway can still be followed on foot and is a pleasant walk on a summer's day. The start is at the site of the tramway terminus adjacent to Monkbretton Bridge on the eastern outskirts of Rye. From here a wide footpath follows the route of the line as far as the site of the bridge over the Broadwater stream. Walkers will need to deviate from the old route here, via the Rye to Camber road, and rejoin it near Gorse Cottage to follow the concreted rails as far as Golf Links Halt Station.

From Golf Links Halt the route to Camber Sands can be followed on an official footpath that cuts across the golf links of Rye Golf Club on a low embankment

PLACES TO VISIT IN RYE
- Landgate Arch
- Ypres Tower - now a museum
- Church of St Mary the Virgin
- Rye Pottery
- Martello tower at Rye Harbour
- Camber Castle
- Royal Military Canal
- Mermaid Inn
- Old Grammar School
- Rye Harbour Nature Reserve

SOUTHWOLD RAILWAY

HALESWORTH TO SOUTHWOLD

Located in a rural part of Suffolk, the market town of Halesworth has for thousands of years been connected by the meandering River Blyth to the fishing port of Southwold, seven miles to east. The river ensured Halesworth's importance as a trading centre well before the Romans settled in the area. In fact, archaeological evidence has shown human habitation in the area stretching back to Stone Age times. By the time the Romans had arrived, Iron Age farming settlements had become firmly established on both banks of the river. It was during the Roman occupation that Halesworth became a well established trading centre, not only because of the river link to the sea but also due to the network of Roman roads that passed through the area.

Halesworth further developed during Saxon times when a church was built on the site of the present St Mary's. The church was expanded to its present size during medieval times under the sponsorship of the Argentein family, who had settled in the area from France after the Norman invasion. Halesworth grew in importance during the 13th century following the granting of a licence to hold a weekly market in the town.

By the 16th century Halesworth, with its ease of access to the sea, had become a wealthy trading centre with an unusually large number of apothecaries - a mix of our modern day chemists and GPs. Halesworth's prosperity continued to grow in the mid-18th century when major improvements, such as new locks and cuts, were made to ease navigation on the River Blyth.

Seven miles to the east as the crow flies, Southwold was already an important fishing port when it was first mentioned in Domesday Book. The herring trade was of particular importance, and Southwold received its town charter from

Left *The current Bailey Bridge over the River Blyth was erected in 1977 to replace an earlier version. The original railway swing bridge was replaced in 1907, but its replacement was demolished in 1942.*

Above *2-4-2 tank locomotive* No.1 Southwold, *here seen at Southwold with a mixed train, was the second locomotive to carry this name. The original* No.1 *was returned to its manufacturers in 1883.*

Henry VII in 1489. A major sea battle was fought just off Southwold in 1672 when a joint British-French fleet fought a Dutch fleet during the opening battle of the Third Anglo–Dutch War. The bloody Battle of Solebay involved over 130 fighting ships but, although hundreds of sailors were killed, its outcome was inconclusive.

Southwold never developed as a major port because of the shifting nature of the Suffolk coastline. The town also suffered a devastating fire in 1659 when most of the wooden buildings were destroyed. The many green areas in the town are fire breaks which date from the period of rebuilding. Southwold has three famous landmarks, including the lighthouse which was built in 1887 in the centre of the town, far away from coastal erosion. The others, also visible from miles around, are the tower of 15th century St Edmunds church and a giant 150,000 gallon water tower. Southwold is still justifiably famous today as the home of Adnams Brewery, which has occupied the same site at Sole Bay since 1660.

Railways first came to the region in the 1850s, with the opening of the East Suffolk Railway from Ipswich to Lowestoft.

Right *The first stop after leaving Halesworth, the site of Wenhaston Station is now commemorated by this metal plaque which depicts Southwold Railway 0-6-2 tank locomotive* No.4 Wenhaston.

HISTORY OF THE RAILWAY

Unfortunately for the people of Southwold, the East Suffolk line had taken a course many miles inland from the coast. The nearest stations were nine miles away at Halesworth and Darsham and the once-daily horsedrawn bus to the latter station proved totally inadequate.

The East Suffolk Railway was incorporated into the Great Eastern Railway in 1862 but, despite requests from the people of Southwold for a connecting branch line, the harbour town's economy was slipping away. Twelve miles to the north, rail-connected Lowestoft was rising in ascendancy as a major fishing port. Southwold

Below *A postcard view of a train from Southwold arriving at Halesworth Station. Here there was a goods transfer shed where shipments from the Southwold Railway were transferred by hand on to Great Eastern Railway wagons.*

HALESWORTH STATION. SOUTHWOLD RAILWAY

8003.

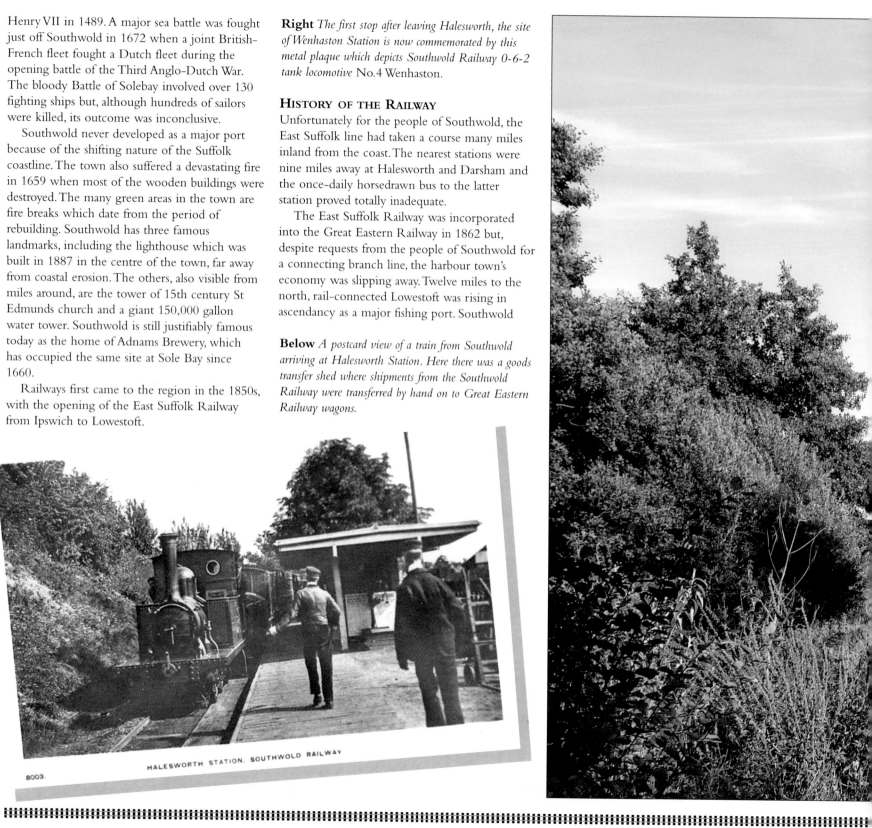

HALESWORTH and SOUTHWOLD.—Southwold.

Sec. and Man., H. Ward, 17, Victoria Street, S.W.

Miles	Down.	Week Days.							Sn
		mrn	mrn	mrn	aft	aft	aft	aft
				1012	1 0	3 18	4 55	4 40
	278 London (L'pool St.).dep	5 0	....					
	Halesworth ....dep.	8 40	1045	1 15	3 45	6 35	8 12	8 0
2½	Wenhaston	8 51	1056	1 26	3 56	6 46	8 23	8 11
5	Blythburgh ‖	9 2	11 7	1 37	4 7	6 57	8 34	8 22
8	Walberswick	9 15	1120	1 50	4 20	7 10	8 47	8 35
9	Southwold ....arr.	9 21	1126	1 56	4 26	7 16	8 53	8 41

Miles	Up.	Week Days.							Sn
		mrn	mrn	mrn	aft	aft	aft	aft
	Southwold ....dep.	7 30	9 45	12 0	2 20	5 23	7 26	5 19
1	Walberswick	7 35	9 50	12 5	2 25	5 28	7 31	5 24
4	Blythburgh ‖	7 49	10 4	1219	2 39	5 42	7 45	5 38
6½	Wenhaston	8 0	1015	1230	2 50	5 53	7 56	5 49
9	Halesworth 278......arr.	8 11	1026	1241	3 1	6 4	8 7	6 0
109½	278 London (L'pool St.) arr.	1122	1 20	3 42	5 56	9 22	....	9 10

‖ Station for Wangford (2¾ miles).

was also missing out on the growth in tourism and trade experienced by other rail-connected coastal towns in Britain.

The residents of Southwold eventually took matters into their own hands and, at a public meeting held in 1875, it was agreed that a narrow gauge line be built to connect the town with Halesworth. An Act of Parliament was passed in 1876 which allowed for the building of a 3ft gauge line but, despite popular local support, insufficient funds had been raised from shareholders for construction work to commence. Finally, following a power struggle in which the Halesworth-based board lost control to city entrepreneurs, work commenced on the line in 1878. With intermediate stations at Wenhaston, Blythburgh and Walberswick. the 8¾-mile line opened for business on 24 September 1879. Motive power was provided by three 2-4-0 tank engines supplied by Sharp, Stewart of

Left *West of Blythburgh it is possible to walk the overgrown trackbed of the Southwold Railway. The tower of Holy Trinity Church can be seen in the distance.* **Inset** *The railway's timetable in 1922.*

Above *Posing with a rather dour member of staff, one of the original 2-4-0 tank locomotives,* No 2 Halesworth *stands at Southwold engine shed, probably just before closure of the line.*

Manchester. They were named No.1 *Southwold*, No.2 *Halesworth* and No. 3 *Blyth*. Due to financial problems, *Southwold* was returned to Sharp, Stewart in 1883 and finally found its way to Colombia. A second *Southwold* was purchased from Sharp, Stewart in 1893. Although similar in most respects to the original locomotives, the second *Southwold* had a 2-4-2 wheel arrangement. In 1916, to deal with the anticipated heavy traffic on the newly opened harbour branch at Southwold, a fourth more powerful 0-6-2 tank locomotive, No.4 *Wenhaston*, was supplied by Manning Wardle.

A total of six passenger coaches were delivered for the opening of the railway. These were of an unusual design, with the body being carried on three 2-wheeled bogies - although the smoothness of the ride, apparently, was not without fault.

The only major engineering work on the line

Southwold Express

Above *Another postcard view of the Southwold Railway, this time depicting a mixed train departing from Southwold for Halesworth. Note the unusual double aspect signal and the young trainspotters.*

was the swing bridge across the River Blyth on the approach to Southwold. It was rebuilt in 1908 at a time when there was a possibility of the line being converted to standard gauge and extended up the coast to Lowestoft. This never materialised, and the bridge was last swung for shipping in 1914. Following closure in 1929, the bridge was destroyed in World War II during the heightened threat of invasion from Germany. A Bailey bridge, carrying footpath and pipeline, was later erected on the original piers of the old bridge.

From the start most of the trains that ran on the Southwold Railway were of the mixed variety, and the timetable usually allowed four trains a day each way with reduced services on Sundays. Single track throughout, the line was worked on the one-engine-in-steam principle and, because of a 16mph speed restriction, the

journey time was a painfully slow 35 minutes.

However, the little railway managed to make a profit until the mid-1920s when competition from road transport finally sealed its fate. In 1900 the railway carried 10,000 passengers and 90,000 tons of minerals. Prior to World War I there had been plans to convert the line to standard gauge and extend it northwards to Lowestoft and westwards to meet the Mid-Suffolk Light Railway in Laxfield. Apart from a short harbour branch at Southwold, none of these plans ever saw the light of day. World War I saw the War Department taking control of the line, which they continued to run until 1921. During the war, the line was not only heavily used for troop movements but, along with the town of Southwold, also became a target for raiding Zeppelins.

The post-war years were difficult times for the Southwold Railway and much fun was poked at the eccentricities of the line in a series of well-

Right *Now a well-maintained footpath, the trackbed traverses marshland after crossing the River Blyth on the approach to Southwold. Near this spot, a branch line was opened to Southwold Harbour in 1914.*

Railway Station, Southwold

known humorous postcards drawn by Reg Carter. However, the introduction of regular motorbus services between Southwold and Halesworth in 1928 quickly brought about the line's demise. With only one week's notice, the Southwold Railway abruptly closed on 11 April 1929. Over the next few years several plans to reopen the line came to nothing. Although closed, the track remained intact until 1941 when it was lifted for scrap to help the war effort. All locomotives and rolling stock had been collected at Halesworth and lay there rotting until also being broken up in 1941. Taking a long time to die, the Southwold Railway Company was not wound up until 1960 and an abandonment order was only granted in the 1990s.

THE LINE TODAY

Although closed nearly 80 years ago, there are still remains and reminders of the Southwold Railway to be found today by the intrepid and inquisitive 'railway detective'. Before we start to explore the route of the Southwold Railway, it is worth visiting the north end of Halesworth main line station to see the unusual swinging platform and level crossing that

Above *Another in the series of railway postcards, this one depicting Edwardian passengers waiting for their train at Southwold while one of the railway's locomotives gets up steam outside the engine shed. Beyond the station is the Station Hotel - today it still stands but has been renamed the Blyth Hotel.*

was built by Boulton & Paul for the Great Eastern Railway in 1888. A relic of days long ago when steam railways reigned supreme, the platform has been recently restored. Now covered by a housing development, nothing now remains of the Southwold Railway terminus at Halesworth, but a short distance south the brick abutments that once carried the line over Holton Road can still be seen. Strangely, although the railway closed in 1929, the steel girders were only removed in the early 1960s. A well-preserved brick arched bridge stands a short distance further down the line and from here it is possible to walk along the old trackbed to the site of the former engine shed. Apart from the brick foundations, nothing now remains of this building. Near Mells, a road bridge known locally as Ball's Bridge is one of the few other structures that have survived fairly well intact – although its width and loading gauge were increased in 1906 to accommodate standard gauge trains, the plan to convert the

Below *The first railway swing bridge across the River Blyth at Southwold was replaced in 1907 by a wider version capable of carrying a standard gauge line. The plan to link the Southwold Railway with the national rail system never transpired and the bridge was demolished during World War II. On the same site, this modern Bailey Bridge carries a footpath and pipeline.*

Southwold Railway never transpired.

Another reminder of the little railway can be found at the site of Wenhaston Station. Here, where the line crossed the road on the level, an attractive commemorative steel plaque depicting locomotive No.4 *Wenhaston*, has been erected to mark the spot. The next station along the line was at Blythburgh, and today very little remains apart from a timber coal shed lurking in the undergrowth between the magnificent medieval Holy Trinity Church and the River Blyth.

Between Blythburgh and the next station,

Walberswick, the trackbed of the Southwold Railway passes through a National Nature Reserve. If you are a horse rider then you will be very pleased as about half of the route is for 'Horse Riders Only'. Sadly, for those of us on Shanks's Pony, we have to take our life in our hands and divert to the B1387 near The Heronry before rejoining the trackbed to the west of Walberswick.

The concrete base of Walberswick Station still remains today where a seat has kindly been provided for the weary walker by the Southwold Railway Society. Don't be misled, as Walberswick Station is some distance from the village of that name! Southwold, with its prominent landmarks of lighthouse, church tower and water tower beckons in the distance. On its approach to the town, the Southwold Railway crossed the River Blyth on a fairly substantial swing bridge, The original structure was replaced in 1907 as part of the failed plan to upgrade the line to standard gauge. The current structure, a Bailey Bridge, still

Above *A short branch line was built to Southwold Harbour in 1914. Although the line has long since disappeared, a short length of rusting track can still be seen at Blackshore Quay opposite the Yacht Club.*

rests on the original supports on each bank of the river.

Just beyond the bridge a short branch line led down to Southwold Harbour. Opened in 1914 very little remains today, but a short length of rusting track can still be seen by Blackshore Quay opposite the Southwold Sailing Club. Reverting

back to the 'main line', the trackbed crosses marshland before entering a cutting prior to making its final approach to Southwold.

A footbridge, made of secondhand rails, was erected across the cutting in 1903 for use by members of the Southwold Golf Club. Demolished in the 1970s, only the concrete bases now remain. The end of the line, Southwold Station, has long since disappeared and in its place is a modern police station. Houses have also been built on the site of the approaches and sidings and even the Station Hotel has changed its name. All

that remains today is a small brass plaque fixed to wall of the police station in commemoration of the little Southwold Railway - Rest In Peace!

But is this really the end of the line?

The Southwold Railway Trust was formed in 1994 with the long term aim to reopen at least part of the line. A consultation document was published in 2003, with the plan to reopen the whole of the route between Southwold and Halesworth. The primary aims of the Trust were to reopen the line as a local transport system, to help manage summer traffic including a park-and-ride scheme and, finally, as a tourist line. Following public consultation a second plan was published in 2005 with an adjusted route. The reopened railway would closely follow the original route from Halesworth to Blythburgh, then head north and continue to Southwold to the north of the River Blyth, finally ending at the refurbished pier. The Trust's planning application for Phase 1, which would open the line from Henman Park to Southwold Pier, was submitted to the local councils in March 2007. Sadly, there was some local opposition and the neither of the District Councils felt able to support the application. The Trust now hopes that a future change in planning laws may make their application to reopen the line a much more likely proposition. We all wish them well!

In the meantime, the Trust is planning to create a Southwold Railway Engine Shed Museum and a full size working replica of one of the Sharp, Stewart 2-4-0 tank locomotives. For further details about the Southwold Railway Trust visit their shop at 27 High Street, Southwold, Suffolk IP18 6AD (tel. 01502 725422) or their website: www.southwoldrailway.co.uk

Above *Easily overlooked on Blackshore Quay, this rusting piece of track is all that remains of the branch line to Southwold Harbour. The branch opened in 1914 but was rarely used, as the promise of regular fresh fish traffic was never fully realised.*

Left *A busy scene at Southwold Station as a train arrives from Halesworth. This early 20th century postcard view is full of Edwardian detail, including the many enamelled metal advertisements on the corrugated iron-roofed building, and the horse-drawn carriages and period costume. A modern police station now occupies this site.*

Above *This small brass plaque is fixed to the wall of the modern police station in Southwold. With a life of nearly 50 years, the Southwold Railway came to an abrupt end in September 1929 when only one week's notice was given of its closure.*

Left *Now a well-signposted footpath, the final approach to Southwold Station was through a cutting that bisected the local golf club. Only demolished in the 1970s, a footbridge was built across the line in 1903 to allow golfers access to the greens.*

ORDNANCE SURVEY MAP

Landranger 1:50,000 series No. 156

TOURIST INFORMATION

Nearest office: Southwold Tourist Information Centre, 69 High Street, Southwold, Suffolk IP18 6DS (tel. 01502 724729) or visit: www.visit-sunrisecoast.co.uk

WHERE TO STAY

There is a wide range of accommodation in Halesworth, Southwold and the surrounding area. For more details contact Southwold Tourist Information Centre (see above).

RAILWAY WALKS

Apart from a few isolated lengths of trackbed that can be walked between Halesworth and Blythburgh (see page 51), the longest section that is designated as a footpath is between the latter village and Southwold via Walberswick. Passing through a National Nature Reserve, part of the trackbed is now for the sole use of horse riders, and walkers have to deviate on to the B1387 between The Heronry and just south of Walberswick. From here it is a fairly pleaseant stroll across the Bailey Bridge over the River Blyth before taking a diversion to Blackshore Quay, where it is still possible to find a short length of track from the Harbour Branch. Retracing our steps to the main line, the trackbed crosses marshland and through a cutting to the site of Southwold railway station - now a police station!

The Southwold Railway Trust have published an excellent ring-bound guide to walks along the Southwold Railway and the Blyth Valley. The guide is divided into two sections: one for eastbound walking to Southwold and one for westbound walking to Halesworth. For further details about the Trust see page 53.

PLACES TO VISIT
- Halesworth & District Museum
- St Mary's Church, Halesworth
- Gun Hill, Southwold
- Southwold Museum
- Southwold Sailors' Reading Rooms
- Southwold Lifeboat Museum
- St Edmund's Church, Southwold

Below *A wonderfully detailed photograph taken at Southwold Station at the beginning of the 20th century. To reduce construction costs, the carriage shed on the right only had one covered side. The small boy may have been dreaming of becoming an engine driver!*

ASHOVER LIGHT RAILWAY

CLAY CROSS TO ASHOVER

Set high in the Derbyshire hills, the upper reaches of the Amber Valley are quite rightly known as the valley of silence and wild flowers. However, it was not always such a silent place, as for many centuries the valley was a flourishing industrial centre with lead mines, quarries, lime kilns, a coal mine, flour mills, nailmakers, stocking frames, basketmakers and rope works. In particular, the picturesque village of Ashover – first mentioned in the Domesday Book – had a history of lead mining and quarrying that dated back to Roman times.

Three miles to the east of Ashover, as the crow flies, is the village of Clay Cross which, until the coming of the North Midland Railway in 1840, was a fairly sleepy place. This all changed when the engineer of the new railway, George Stephenson, discovered rich seams of coal during the excavation of Clay Cross Tunnel. With local sources of limestone and ironstone also available, Stephenson set up a company not only to mine the coal but also to erect blast furnaces for the manufacture of iron. Later known as the Clay Cross Company, it became one of the largest private companies in Britain.

Left *Perfectly preserved in its original condition, the corrugated iron station building at Fallgate is now on private land. The owners have even laid a short length of 2ft gauge track to await the reopening of the line.*

Below *These buildings are all that now remain of the once mighty Clay Cross Company. Once one of the largest private companies in Britain, it was taken over in 1985 but closed in 2000 with the loss of 700 jobs.*

Above 4-6-0 tank locomotive Hummy, *here seen at Clay Cross in the 1930s, was built by the Baldwin Locomotive Company of Philadelphia for service on the Western Front in World War I.*

HISTORY OF THE RAILWAY

By 1913 the Clay Cross Company had come under the control of William Jackson, and the company had expanded its operations to include a brickworks, three blast furnaces, a foundry, coke ovens and a gas plant, seven coal mines, a limestone quarry and limeworks and several ironstone mines. The company was keen to further expand its operations.

Just over half a mile south of Ashover lies Overton Hall, once the home of the famous scientist and naturalist Sir Joseph Banks. By 1918 the estate, which not only included the parish of Ashover but also valuable untapped mineral deposits such as limestone, fluorspar, gritstone and

Right This brick abutment is all that remains of the famous 'Pirelli Bridge' that took the Ashover Light Railway across the Chesterfield road at Clay Cross. The bridge was removed in 1951.

Right *A Gloucester Railway Carriage & Wagon Company passenger coach, supplied new to the Ashover Light Railway in 1922, waits for passengers at the unprepossessing northern terminus of the line at Clay Cross. The line carried on for a further ½-mile beyond the station to serve various parts of the Clay Cross Company's works.*

Below *After Clay Cross and Chesterfield Road stations, Holmgate halt was the third stop on the journey to Ashover. Holmgate had a small wooden shelter and a short siding. Today the route of the line to the north of Holmgate Road is partly obscured by trees.*

Left *In 1959, nine years after the closure of the Ashover Light Railway, the North Derbyshire Water Board flooded part of the valley between Brackenfield and Woolley to form a reservoir. As a result about a mile of the old trackbed is now submerged.*

barytes, came up for sale. Realising that a rail link from Clay Cross was vital for the removal of these deposits, the Clay Cross Company first gained permission to build a railway across the land of the neighbouring Ogston Hall estate before purchasing the Overton Estate in 1919. Everything was now in place for the building of the Ashover Light Railway.

Prior to the purchase of the Overton Estate by the Clay Cross Company, there had been several plans to build a standard gauge railway up the Amber Valley from a junction with the Midland Railway at Stretton, just south of Clay Cross. One of these routes had already been surveyed by Colonel H F Stephens and a Light Railway Order had been granted. Nothing came of these plans until 1919, when one of the routes already surveyed by Stephens was chosen for the Ashover Light Railway. To reduce

construction costs, a gauge of 2ft was chosen for the circuitous seven mile route from the Clay Cross Works to Ashover via Stretton and the Ogston Estate. Although construction of the line was put out to tender, the Clay Cross Company decided to construct the line itself. Initially the Company had not planned to operate passenger services but, by 1922 when the Light Railway Order was eventually approved, it was obvious that the scenic delights of the Amber Valley could generate extra traffic during the summer months.

It was fortunate for the Clay Cross Company that a large number of war surplus steam locomotives, wagons and 60cm gauge track, supplied for use in France during World War I, were up for sale at this time. Four Baldwin 4-6-0 steam tank engines were purchased at a knock-down price and subsequently named after the four children of General Jackson, one of the directors of the Company. They were *Peggy, Joan,*

Below *Four new bogie carriages were ordered from the Gloucester Railway Carriage & Wagon Company and delivered to the Ashover Light Railway in 1924. Here No. 1, resplendent in the ALR livery of crimson lake with black shaded gold letters, poses for a works photo.*

PASSENGER CARRIAGE, ASHOVER LIGHT RY.

3

Guy and *Hummy* and, by 1922, were in use on various sections of the line during its construction. At the same time, 50 bogie open wagons were also purchased from the War Stores Disposals Board and four new passenger carriages were supplied by the Gloucester Railway Carriage & Wagon Company. The only major engineering works on the line were restricted to the Clay Cross end, where a half-mile embankment with a gradient of 1 in 37 was built to take the line on a girder bridge across the Chesterfield road. The bridge was soon adorned with an advert for Pirelli Tyres and became known locally as 'The Pirelli Bridge'. With contruction finished and amidst much ceremony, the Ashover Light Railway was officially opened on 6 April 1925, when two special trains decorated with flags and bunting took 120 guests to a luncheon at Ashover.

The newly opened line was an immediate hit with day trippers, especially at weekends and on Bank Holidays. The four passenger carriages were insufficient to cope with the demand, so eight further carriages were purchased in 1926 from the Neverstop Railway that had been operating at the British Empire Exhibition in Wembley. By this date *Guy* was worn out, so two more Baldwin locomotives were purchased from the War Stores Disposal Board. One was named *Bridget* and the other received the nameplates

Right *Situated close to the wooded banks of the River Amber, the site of Dalebank station is an idyllic spot in summer. The Ashover Light Railway Society have long term plans to reopen part of the railway and build a new station here.*

from the original *Guy*, which by then had been withdrawn.

Also by the summer of 1926 a wooden cafe, named 'Where the Rainbow Ends', was opened at the picturesque terminus of the line at The Butts, Ashover. Featured on many postcards of the line, the cafe was a great hit with day-trippers and was easily recognised by its rainbow coloured roof tiles.

However, the Ashover Light Railway was initially built as a freight line to carry minerals from the quarries at Ashover, Fallgate and Milltown to the Clay Cross Works and, apart from busy weekend and holiday periods, the goods wagons carrying the stone traffic were attached to the rear of weekday passenger trains.

The summer of 1927 saw the peak of passenger services on the Ashover Light Railway and, by the following year, direct motor bus services from Chesterfield to Ashover were making an impact on passenger numbers. The decline continued and, by 1936, all regular passenger services were withdrawn. Goods traffic, also affected by competition

THE CLAY CROSS COMPANY

Originally a small hamlet known as Clay Lane, the area around Clay Cross in Derbyshire has been a centre for coal mining since the 17th century. During the construction of the North Midland Railway in 1838 the engineer of the new line, George Stephenson, discovered rich seams of coal during the excavation of Clay Cross Tunnel. A new company, known as Geo Stephenson & Co, quickly set about coal mining operations and was soon supplying the North Midland railway with coke for its locomotives. In 1844, it became the first company to transport coal by rail to London and, in 1846, opened two blast furnaces. George Stephenson died in 1848 and was succeeded by his son Robert, who only remained as Chairman until 1852, when the company was taken over by Henry Morton Peto, Joshua Walmsley and William Jackson. It was at this stage that the company name was changed to The Clay Cross Company. By 1871 William Jackson had become sole owner of the company and, within a few years, had expanded it to become one of the largest private companies in Britain. By 1913 The Clay Cross Company's operations included seven collieries, a limeworks, a limestone quarry, ironstone mines, a brickworks, three blast furnaces, a foundry, coke ovens and a gas plant. The company was taken over by Biwater in 1985, but was closed in 2000 with the loss of over 700 jobs.

Left *Backing on to the River Amber, the original corrugated iron station building at Fallgate and a short length of recently laid track wait patiently for the proposed reopening of the Ashover Light Railway between Ogston Reservoir and Ashover.*

from road lorries, also declined but the little line struggled on through World War II.

By 1950 the railway was worn out – the track was in a very bad state of repair and there were only two serviceable steam locomotives. The end came when the quarry at The Butts, which had been producing ballast for British Railways, finally closed. One of the last railways to be built in Britain and after only 25 years of life, the Ashover Light Railway finally closed on 31 March 1950.

Apart from an isolated short section of track at Fallgate, which was kept in situ until 1969 to serve a fluorspar quarry, the railway had been completely dismantled by September 1951.

THE LINE TODAY

Although the Ashover Light Railway was short-lived and has been closed for nearly 60 years, there are still a few tantalising clues to the line's existence that can be discovered today. The Clay Cross Company's works are now closed but, although the famous Pirelli Bridge across the Chesterfield road at Clay Cross has also long since gone, one of its brick abutments still stands. The embankment behind it and the site of Chesterfield Road station are now completely overgrown and difficult to access.

With a little bit of detective work, the route of the line can still be seen at Holmgate and also at Stretton. Further south, it disappears beneath the waters of Ogston reservoir which was completed in 1959. At Woolley, however, the line of the low embankment can still be seen in times of drought when the water levels are lower. There are even people of an indeterminate age who live around here that can still remember travelling on the line before it closed in 1950!

Right *Preserved in concrete is this set of 2ft gauge points that lead into the quarry at Fallgate. Some of the trackwork at Fallgate, together with wagons and a diesel locomotive, were kept in use until 1969.*

Further up the Amber Valley, the sites of both Dalebank and Milltown stations can also be found with the aid of a good map and a bit of detective work. The popular Miners Arms pub is located adjacent to the site of the latter station and, a further quarter mile further west, the corrugated iron station building at Fallgate is the *pièce de resistance* of our voyage of discovery. Perfectly preserved in its original condition, the station building currently lies on private land and is graced with a short length of recently laid 2ft gauge track.

Since the closure of the quarries in 1969 much of the land around Fallgate has been landscaped, and it is now hard to imagine the once bustling scene. The former quarry office is now a private home, but a short walk past this building will take us up to the quarry where a short section of 2ft gauge track and a set of points have been preserved forever in the concreted road.

Below *An idyllic postcard view of the Amber Valley at The Butts, Ashover. A train from Clay Cross can be seen approaching in the distance. As no turntable was provided here, trains turned on the triangle seen in the foreground.*

Crossing over the narrowing River Amber in several places, the route of the line between Fallgate and Salter Lane station (for Ashover) runs along a low embankment and is fairly easy to spot. The former terminus of the line at The Butts and site of the 'Where the Rainbow Ends' cafe lies a further half mile west of Ashover. A quiet spot on a summer's day, it is still easy to imagine a train disgorging its load of day trippers in the late 1920s when the line was in its short heyday.

Fortunately this is not the end of the line for the Ashover Light Railway! In 1996, a group of enthusiasts established the Ashover Light Railway Society and they are currently aiming to reopen the 2½-mile section of line between The Butts at Ashover and Dark Lane on the B6014 close to Ogston Reservoir. To extend beyond this to Clay Cross would involve major engineering works as part of the route now lies under water. The Society's plans include a headquarters, car park, cafe and shop at a new station that would be located near the original ALR station at Woolley. Intermediate stations at Dalebank, Milltown,

Above *In October 1926, just over a year after the opening of the Ashover Light Railway,* Joan *and* Gloucester *carriage No. 3 wait at The Butts, Ashover. Behind the train a horse-drawn cart is being loaded with coal from an ex-War Department wagon.*

AMBER VALE FROM THE BUTTS, ASHOVER.

Right *Named after General Jackson's son, Henry Humphrey Jackson,* Hummy *was one of the first batch of four ex-War Department Baldwin locomotives to be delivered to the Ashover Light Railway in 1923.* Hummy *was withdrawn in 1946 and scrapped in 1951.*

Fallgate (where the original station still survives) and Salter Lane would also be reopened.

The Society also plans to reinstate the original 'Where the Rainbow Ends' cafe at the Butts. The cafe was dismantled in 1950 after the closure of the line and rebuilt at the Clay Cross Company's sports field in Clay Cross, where it was joined by ALR carriage No. 4 (minus bogies). The cafe was reopened in 1952 and was in use until 2007 when the current owners of the site, Maximus, decided to redevelop the land. Fortunately, the Society were able to negotiate with the owners so that the cafe could be moved back to The Butts. The building was dismantled in November 2007 and is currently waiting to be returned to its original home.

For more details about the Ashover Light Railway Society visit their website: www.alrs.org.uk

Below *An official postcard view of the 'Where the Rainbow Ends' cafe at The Butts near Ashover. The wooden building was prefabricated at the Clay Cross Works and opened for business on Whit Sunday, 1926. The cafe boasted monogrammed crockery and waitress service.*

Above *Today, the approach to the site of the station at The Butts is hidden deep in undergrowth. Out of the picture to the right is Marsh Brook which was crossed by the railway on a small bridge. Although an enormous success with day trippers for a few years after opening in 1925, increased competition from motor buses soon brought about the end of passenger services on the Ashover Light Railway.*

ORDNANCE SURVEY MAP
Landranger 1:50,000 series No. 119

TOURIST INFORMATION
Matlock: Matlock Tourist Information Centre, Crown Square, Matlock, Derbyshire DE4 3AT (tel. 01629 583388)
Chesterfield: Chesterfield Tourist Information Centre, the Peacock Centre, Lower Pavement, Chesterfield, Derbyshire S40 1PB (tel. 01246 345777)
For either of the above also visit website: www.peakdistrictonline.co.uk

WHERE TO STAY
For accommodation in the upper Amber Valley contact either Matlock or Chesterfield Tourist Information Centres (see above).

RAILWAY WALKS
The trackbed of the old Ashover Light Railway is now privately owned and permission should first be sought before attempting to walk along any part of its length between Clay Cross and Ashover. However, it is still possible to access the former quarry at Fallgate where 2ft gauge track is concreted into the road. The site of the old terminus, turning triangle and quarry at The Butts is also accessible on foot through a gate from the B6036 just west of Ashover.

PLACES TO VISIT
● Tramway Museum, Crich
● Hardwick Hall
● Bolsover Castle
● Tramway Museum, Crich
● Ogston Reservoir
● Miners Arms Inn, Milltown
Ashover:
● Site of old Druid temple on The Fabric
● All Saints Church
● Church of All Saints
● 14th century Crispin Inn
● Black Swan pub

TERMINUS OF ASHOVER LIGHT RAILWAY AT THE BUTTS, ASHOVER.

Right *Another of the official postcard views of the Ashover Light Railway showing the passenger terminus at The Butts, Ashover in 1926. A siding to a small coal yard, office and weighbridge can be seen to the left of the station. A small and short-lived ice cream hut is immediately behind the station. In the top right is The Butts Methodist Chapel and the road leading up to Ashover village.*

LEEK & MANIFOLD VALLEY LIGHT RAILWAY

WATERHOUSES TO HULME END

The River Manifold flows for 12 miles through the limestone hills of the Peak District in Staffordshire from its source south of Buxton, before joining the River Dove near the village of Thorpe in Derbyshire. During dry periods the river disappears underground between Wetton and Ilam. The Manifold's main tributary, the River Hamps, joins it near Beeston Tor.

With its dramatic limestone cliffs and caves, the secluded Manifold Valley also has a fascinating industrial past. Copper and lead have been mined around the village of Ecton since the 16th century, and in 1760 the landowner, the Duke of Devonshire, opened a large copper mine on Ecton Hill. Within a few years, the mine was one of the largest in Britain, producing around 4,000 tons of copper ore a year. The demand was so great that the Duke also opened his own smelter in the nearby Churnet Valley. Lead ore was also mined locally and transported by pack horse and canal to Hull on the East Coast. By the early 19th century the ore in the mine was almost exhausted but, although the Duke had by now lost interest, small scale mining continued until the 1890s.

Until the opening of the nearby Cromford Canal in 1794, raw materials were transported across the difficult terrain of the Peak District by packhorse. Although the canal was an immediate success, it was the opening of railways during the 19th century that made the biggest impact. The two major towns in the region, Leek and Buxton,

were first served by rail in 1849 and 1863 respectively. To the southeast, Ashbourne did not get a rail connection until 1894. The opening of these lines transformed the region and introduced, for the first time, the beauty of the Peak District to a much wider audience. Thus began a new era of tourism which still plays a vital economic role in the region today.

Left *The northern end of the Leek & Manifold Valley Light Railway at Ecton today. The 8-mile trackbed is now a popular tarmacked footpath and cyclepath known as the Manifold Way.*

Above *The Leek & Manifold only possessed four passenger coaches. The intricate cast-iron balconies at each end were a throwback to the railway's chief engineer's previous career on Indian railways.*

HISTORY OF THE LINE

Once an important centre for mining, by the end of the 19th century the Manifold Valley had become a quiet backwater. By now dairy farming was the order of the day, and ways were sought to convey milk to a much wider market. No road ran along its length, however, and its sleepy villages and farms, set high above the valley floor, were difficult to access. Although nearby Leek had been served by the North Staffordshire Railway since 1849, it was still a slow process to transport dairy produce from the Manifold Valley to that town. By 1894, the London & North Western Railway had opened its railway between Buxton and Ashbourne and thus created a quicker and alternative route for the export of local produce. The people of Leek were so alarmed at this potential loss of business that the local MP, Charles Bill, proposed the building of a railway from Leek to the Manifold Valley. In a very unique arrangement, a plan was put forward for two railways, one standard gauge and one narrow gauge, to be built by two separate companies, the North Staffordshire Railway and the Leek & Manifold Valley Light Railway. To add to the confusion, both lines were to be run by the NSR!

In 1899 a Light Railway Order was approved by Parliament for the construction of a 9½-mile standard gauge railway from Leek to Waterhouses, and an 8-mile 2ft 6in narrow gauge line from Waterhouses to Hulme End, near the village of Hartington. Both lines were to be operated by steam locomotives with only minimal station

facilities for passengers. With a successful career of building light railways in India, the innovative Everard Richard Calthrop was appointed consultant engineer for the Leek & Manifold. John B. Earle was appointed resident engineer. Due to ongoing financial problems, construction of the line did not start until 1902. Motive power was provided by two 2-6-4 tank locomotives that were ordered from the Leeds company of Kitson & Co. They were named No. 1 *E. R. Calthrop* and No. 2 *J. B. Earle*. Rolling stock was kept to a minimum - four bogie passenger carriages and eight goods wagons were deemed enough for traffic on the line. The latter included four unique transporter wagons designed by E R Calthrop for conveying standard gauge wagons along the line, thus avoiding time consuming transshipment of goods between the two gauges at Waterhouses. To accommodate the standard gauge wagons, short sections of standard gauge track were laid at the end of sidings at stations along the line.

Although opening of the Leek & Manifold line was planned for 27 June 1904, the standard gauge branch from Leek to Waterhouses was behind schedule and did not open for traffic until July 1905. In the intervening period, steam-powered motor buses operated the connecting service.

Construction of the Leek & Manifold line had involved building over 20 bridges across the Rivers Hamps and Manifold, as well as the 150yd Swainsley Tunnel. A total of seven intermediate stations and halts were located between Waterhouses and Hulme End and all had facilities for the collection and delivery of milk churns - the *raison d'etre* of the line. Hulme End was the principal station on the line with an engine shed and a carriage shed.

Sadly, the Leek & Manifold never quite lived up to its promoter's expectations and ran at a financial loss from the start. Apart from frenzied activity on Bank Holidays, when hundreds of day trippers descended on the line, passenger traffic was very light. The main source of revenue came from transporting milk, either in churns or in standard gauge milk tanks carried on the transporter wagons. The importance of this traffic can be judged by the fact that an overnight milk train was introduced in 1907 between Waterhouses and London. The opening of a

Above *Following closure of the Leek & Manifold in 1934, the line lay dormant for three years until track lifting began in February 1937. No. 1 E. R. Calthrop was steamed once more to assist in the operation.*

Right *Following road widening, most of the station site at Waterhouses has now disappeared. However, the former North Staffordshire Railway goods shed has been restored and is now a convenient cycle hire shop for visitors to the Manifold Way.*

LEEK, WATERHOUSES, and HULME END.—North Staffordshire.

Third class only between Leek and Waterhouses.

Miles		Week Days. mrn (Saturdays only.)	mrn (Saturdays only.)	aft (Wednesdays and Saturdays.)	aft	aft	Suns. aft
	Leek .... dep.	9 5	11 0	1 55	4 35	7 15	3 35
3½	Bradnop	9 16	1111	2 6	4 46	7 26	3 46
5½	Ipstones ¶	9 23	1118	2 13	4 53	7 33	3 53
9¾	Waterhouses .... arr.	9 35	1130	2 25	5 5	7 45	4 5
	Waterhouses .... dep.	9 50	1150	2 35	5 30	8 20	5 5
11¾	Sparrowlee	9 56	1156	2 41	5 36	8 26	5 11
13¼	Beeston Tor	10 4	12 4	2 49	5 44	8 34	5 19
13½	Grindon	10 7	12 7	2 52	5 47	8 37	5 22
14½	Thor's Cave *	1012	1212	2 57	5 52	8 42	5 27
15	Redhurst	a	a	a	a	a	a
15¼	Wetton Mill	1016	1216	3 1	5 56	8 46	5 31
16¾	Butterton	1023	1223	3 8	6 3	8 53	5 38
17	Ecton, for Warslow	1026	1226	3 11	6 6	8 56	5 41
18	Hulme End † .... arr.	1030	1230	3 15	6 10	9 0	5 45

Miles		Week Days. mrn	mrn (Saturdays only.)	mrn (Saturdays only.)	aft (Wednesdays and Saturdays.)	aft	aft	Suns. aft
	Hulme End .... dep.		8 55	1050	1 25	4 5	7 5	3 40
1	Ecton, for Warslow		8 59	1054	1 29	4 14	7 14	3 44
1¼	Butterton		9 2	1057	1 32	4 17	7 17	3 47
2¾	Wetton Mill		9 9	11 4	1 39	4 24	7 24	3 54
3	Redhurst		a	a	a	a	a	a
3½	Thor's Cave *		9 13	11 8	1 43	4 28	7 28	3 58
4½	Grindon		9 18	1113	1 48	4 33	7 33	4 3
4¾	Beeston Tor		9 21	1116	1 51	4 36	7 36	4 6
6¼	Sparrowlee		9 29	1124	1 59	4 44	7 44	4 14
8¼	Waterhouses ¶ .... arr		9 35	1130	2 5	4 50	7 50	4 20
	Waterhouses ¶ .... dep.		9 45	1140	2 35	5 15	8 30	4 50
12½	Ipstones	7 10	9 59	1154	2 49	5 29	8 44	5 6
14¼	Bradnop	7 15	10 5	12 0	2 55	5 35	8 50	5 15
18	Leek 600, 601, 604 ... arr.	7 32	1015	1210	3 5	5 45	9 0	5 25

a Stops when required.
* Station for Wetton.

† Station for Sheen (1⅓ miles) and Hartington (1¾ miles)

¶ "Halts" at Winkhill and Caldon Low between Ipstones and Waterhouses.

Waterhouses Tickets are available at Caldon Low Halt.

creamery at Ecton in 1920, famous for its Stilton cheese, certainly helped to boost traffic but by 1923, when the North Staffordshire Railway and the Leek & Manifold had become part of the mighty London Midland & Scottish, the writing was already on the wall. Light railways all over the country were in terminal decline due to increased competition from road transport, and the Leek & Manifold was no exception. The final nail in the coffin came in 1932, when the conveyance of all milk traffic from the Manifold Valley was transferred to road haulage. The end was near and, less than 30 years after the opening of the line, the LMS announced that the last train would run on 10 March 1934. Not many local people mourned its passing. With its narrow gauge feeder gone, the Leek to Waterhouses standard gauge line closed to passengers 18 months later, and completely in 1943.

With its track, stations and rolling stock frozen

Left *Looking north along the Manifold Way from the site of Grindon station. At nearby Weags Bridge the Leek & Manifold encountered its first road crossing for three miles since crossing the A52 at Waterhouses.*

Above *One of the many official postcards produced by the North Staffordsire Railway extolling the beautiful scenery encountered on the Leek & Manifold. Here, a train bound for Waterhouses passes Darfur Crags as it approaches Wetton Mill.*

in time, the Leek & Manifold slumbered on until early 1937 when demolition contractors started lifting the track. Amazingly, No. 1 *E. R. Calthrop* was given the kiss of life and steamed for the last time to haul the track-lifting train, but was ignominiously cut-up once its job was completed. The other locomotive, No. 2 *J. B. Earle,* had been transferred to Crewe Works on closure of the line, but was also scrapped in 1937.

Although the short-lived Leek & Manifold was now gone, its memories lived on! The LMS gave the trackbed to Staffordshire County Council, who opened it as a footpath in July 1937. A section of the footpath through Swainsley Tunnel was upgraded to a road in the 1950s, and the whole 8-mile route has since been tarmacked throughout. Popular with cyclists and walkers, it is now known as the Manifold Way.

THORS CAVE, MANIFOLD VALLEY
(North Stafford Railway)

Above *The scenic attractions of the Leek & Manifold are very evident here in this official NSR postcard. One of the line's biggest attractions, Thor's Cave, towers 250ft above the little railway. Excavations in the cave show that it was occupied over 10,000 years ago.*

THE LINE TODAY

Now a cycletrack and footpath known as the Manifold Way, the 8-mile route of the Leek & Manifold Valley Light Railway passes through some of the most spectacular scenery in northern England. The start or finish of the route can be at either end of the line, as both Waterhouses and Hulme End have car parking, toilets, refreshment and picnic facilities.

During the period when the little railway was operating, most passengers would have arrived at Waterhouses after their train journey from Stoke-on-Trent and Leek. Today much of the station site has long since disappeared following road widening, but the North Staffordshire Railway bridge which once carried the standard gauge line to Leek still stands proudly across the road to Cauldon. The only building still standing is the former NSR goods shed which is now a cycle hire centre and cafe. From here the route soon descends to the busy A52, which the line once crossed on the level. Once across the road, it is fairly plain sailing to follow the route of the line along the tarmacked cycleway that runs along the valley bottoms of the Rivers Hamps and Manifold. The rivers are crossed many times by the bridges that were originally erected for the railway, but little now remains of any of the intermediate stations.

It soon becomes obvious to anyone walking or cycling along the Manifold Way that while the little railway passed through some of the best scenery in England, it did not exactly pass through any populated areas – in fact the villages it served were usually one mile away at the top of the valley. This factor certainly contributed to the railway's early death.

Right *Located in a steep limestone crag, Thor's Cave is still a major tourist attraction today. Access from the Manifold Way is via a steep permissive footpath on land owned by the National Trust. Sadly, the old wooden tea room and station building are no more.*

E R CALTHROP

Born in 1857, Everard Richard Calthrop was the son of a Lincolnshire farmer. Calthrop started his railway engineering career as an apprentice with Robert Stephenson & Co and the L&NWR at Crewe. At the age of 22 he joined the GWR, where he soon became assistant manager at their Swindon Carriage & Wagon Works. Three years later, he joined the Great Indian Peninsular Railway as a locomotive inspector before returning to Britain, where he became a consultant railway engineer in 1892. An innovative man, Calthrop was responsible for the building of the Barsi Light Railway and the Matheran Light Railway – both in India – as well as other narrow gauge lines in Burma, Australia and Barbados. He is best known in Britain as consultant engineer for the Leek & Manifold Valley Light Railway. Calthrop died in 1927.

Above *A quiet moment at Ecton in between shunting operations. The passengers in the carriage on the right wait patiently for the locomotive to return from its duties, to resume their journey to Hulme End. One of E. R. Calthrop's innovative transporter wagons with its standard gauge van can be seen in the siding.*

Right *A long way from home! A GWR covered van sits piggy back on one of the Leek & Manifold's transporter wagons at Hulme End on 12 August 1933 - only seven months before closure of the line.*

Left *A form of Edwardian NIMBYism, the 154yd Swainsley Tunnel was built so that the Leek & Manifold could not spoil the view from Swainsley Hall. Coincidentally, Swainsley Hall was owned by one of the railway's directors, Sir Thomas Wardle! Unfortunately, this northern section of the Manifold Way is also used by cars.*

Above *Looking south along the Manifold Way from the site of Ecton station. On Ecton Hill to the east are the former copper mines that brought enormous wealth to the Duke of Devonshire in the late 18th century. Ecton Hill is now owned by the National Trust.*

Leaving Waterhouses behind, the Manifold Way closely follows the River Hamps, crossing the river no less than 14 times before reaching the site of Beeston Tor station. With little or no local traffic to speak of, this station was popular with summer day trippers who would alight here to visit Beeston Tor Cave. It was here in 1924 that a local vicar discovered a Saxon hoard of coins and jewellery that dated back to the 9th century. The station was busy enough to warrant a refreshment room, but its wooden structure has long since gone. Just north of Beeston Tor the River Hamps joins the River Manifold and, during the summer months, this stretch of river is usually dry as its course lies underground as far as Wetton Mill. At Weags Bridge the Manifold Way crosses the Grindon to Hopedale road - the first such road crossing since the A52 at Waterhouses. The site of Grindon station is now used as a car park.

With limestone crags towering over the valley, this section of the Manifold Way is the most scenic on the route. A short distance north of Grindon lies the site of Thor's Cave station - so named after the enormous cave that overlooks the valley. Thor's Cave was probably the most popular destination on the Leek & Manifold, and a wooden refreshment room once existed here to quench the thirst of visitors who had made the steep climb up the side of the valley to the cave.

Located 250ft above the valley floor, Thor's Cave is 30ft high, 23ft wide and the roof is supported by massive limestone columns. Stone tools and the bones of extinct mammals which have been excavated here show that the cave was probably inhabited by Stone Age man over 10,000 years ago.

Left *Taken soon after the opening of the line, this photograph shows the original livery of the Leek & Manifold locomotives and carriages. The 2-6-4 tank locomotives were painted a light chocolate brown with white lining, while the carriages were attractively finished in primrose yellow and black lining..*

Below *End of the line! A quiet day at Hulme End in August 1933, only seven months before closure. Not much seems to be happening, which was the order of the day during the little railway's death throes. The loss of vital milk traffic to road transport in 1932 was the final nail in the railway's coffin.*

A short distance north of Thor's Cave, the Manifold Way becomes a road for the next 1½ miles. At Wetton Mill, the site of the station is now a car park catering for the large number of visitors who descend on this usually tranquil valley on summer weekends. Wetton Mill dates back to the 17th century but has long ceased to grind corn. A tea room here caters for the thirsty walker or cyclist.

North of Wetton Mill, the Manifold Way continues along a tarmacked road before passing through Swainsley Tunnel. Butterton station, now a car park, is reached soon after emerging from the tunnel. Nearing the end of the line, Ecton is now unrecognisable from its heyday as a rail-connected milk factory and creamery in the early 20th century. The transferral of this important milk traffic from the Leek & Manifold to road transport in 1932 spelled the end for the railway. Even the scars from centuries of copper mining on Ecton Hill (now National Trust) are being taken over by nature. Now all is peace and quiet.

Leaving the road behind, the final mile of the Manifold Way completes its journey to Hulme End as a dedicated footpath and cyclepath. The end of the line at Hulme End is now a pleasant picnic site with car parking. The former station building has been beautifully restored and the ticket office now houses the Manifold Visitor Centre. An information service is available here most weekends and during school holidays. There is also a permanent exhibition of the history of the railway, the local archaeology and natural history of the Manifold Valley. Adjacent to the station building, the former engine shed has been completely rebuilt. Just beyond the station is a 200-year-old coaching inn - 'The Manifold Inn', formerly the 'The Light Railway' - where weary walkers and cyclists can restore their energy.

The village of Hulme End is the end of the line and its size gives credence to a local saying: that the Leek & Manifold Valley Light Railway was 'A line starting nowhere and ending up at the same place'!

Left *At the northern end of the Manifold Way, the station building at Hulme End has been beautifully restored and now houses the Manifold Visitor Centre with its permanent exhibition of the railway's history.*

Below *Hulme End station shortly before closure. Again, nothing much seems to be happening! The old NSR standard gauge carriage, minus wheels, provided basic facilities for a cycle shed and store.*

ORDNANCE SURVEY MAP
Landranger 1:50,000 series No. 119

TOURIST INFORMATION
Ashbourne: Ashbourne Tourist Information Centre, 13 Market Place, Ashbourne, Derbyshire DE6 1EU (tel. 01335 343666)
Buxton: Buxton Tourist Information Centre, The Crescent, Buxton, Derbyshire SK17 6BQ (tel. 01298 25106)
For either of the above centres also visit: www.visitpeakdistrict.com
Leek: Leek Tourist Information Centre, 1 Market Place, Leek, Staffordshire Moorlands ST13 5HH (tel. 01538 483741) or visit: www.staffsmoorlands.gov.uk

WHERE TO STAY
There is a wide range of accommodation, from luxury hotels and inns to bed and breakfast, self-catering establishments and campsites in this part of the Peak District National Park. For more details contact the local Tourist Information Centres (see above).

RAILWAY WALK
Now known as the Manifold Way, the 8-mile trackbed of the Leek & Manifold Valley Light Railway was donated by its then owner, the London Midland & Scottish Railway, to Staffordshire County Council in 1937. The first such public way of its kind in Britain, it is now tarmacked throughout and, apart from a two mile stretch between Wetton Mill and Ecton, is totally dedicated to horse riders, cyclists and walkers. Cycle hire is available at Waterhouses.

PLACES TO VISIT
● Tissington Trail
● High Peak Trail
● Monsal Trail
● Chatsworth House
● Alton Towers
● Kedleston Hall
● The Crescent, Buxton
● Manifold Valley Visitor Centre
● Thor's Cave
● Rudyard Lake Steam Railway
● Ilam Estate Country Park (NT)

GLYN VALLEY TRAMWAY

CHIRK TO GLYN CEIRIOG

Rising in the remote Berwyn Mountains, the River Ceiriog flows down the secluded Ceiriog Valley for a distance of 18 miles until it meets the River Dee near the English-Welsh border, two miles northeast of the town of Chirk. Once described by Lloyd George as 'a little bit of heaven on Earth' this idyllic valley, also known as 'Little Switzerland', with its numerous small farms and forestry plantations, remains relatively unspoilt as it is bypassed by the main tourist route which lies a few miles to the north in the Vale of Llangollen. Steeped in history, folklore and legend the valley was supposedly the setting for a major battle between Henry II's army and the Welsh in the 12th century. Later, the Ceiriog Valley became an important route for Welsh drovers taking their cattle to the English markets. It was also the birthplace of three notable Welsh poets: Huw Morus, Rev Robert Elis and John Ceiriog

Hughes, and home to the novelist Islwyn Ffowc Elis. In more recent times, mystery still surrounds the supposed crash of an enormous flying saucer high up in the Berwyn Mountains to the west of Glyn Ceiriog in 1974. Investigations are still continuing to locate the crash site!

However, the head of the valley around the village of Glyn Ceiriog was once a very different place. Slate had been quarried here since the 16th century but, with the coming of the Industrial Revolution in the early 19th century, what was once a localised affair should have quickly grown into a full-blown industry. The opening of the Ellesmere Canal to Chirk in 1799 increased the prospects of exporting the slate to a much larger market, but there still remained the problem of transporting it along the six miles between the quarries at Glyn Ceiriog and the canal.

Left *Named after the engineer of the Glyn Valley Tramway, Henry Dennis,* Dennis - *here seen at Chirk engine shed on 30 May 1932 - was built by Beyer Peacock of Manchester in 1889.*

Below *The Glyn Valley Tramway engine shed at Chirk in May 1932. Less than a year later all passenger services had ceased running and by July 1935 the line had completely closed.*

HISTORY OF THE RAILWAY

Even though the Ellesmere Canal had opened to Chirk in 1799, it was not until the mid-19th century, by which time the main line railway had also reached the town, that serious plans were put forward for a tramway linking Chirk with the slate quarries around Glyn Ceiriog. In 1857, the Cambrian Slate Company was formed to exploit these quarries commercially, and proposed a horse-drawn tramway to run alongside a new turnpike road down the valley to connect with the Great Western Railway railway south of Chirk, and a nearby wharf with the Ellesmere Canal. The engineering consultant employed by the Cambrian Slate Company was Henry Dennis, who had already been responsible for the building of a tramway from slate quarries in the Dee Valley to link with the Ellesmere Canal.

Left *North of Chirk station and parallel to the present main railway line, the route of the Glyn Valley Tramway extension to the Shropshire Union Canal at the former Blackpark Canal Basin can still be followed today through this woodland.*

Above *Chirk mainline station today. The Glyn Valley Tramway route and site of the tramway's station is now hidden in the woodland behind the present station building. The only road bridge over the GVT route can still be seen today at this location.*

Below *Apart from Bank Holiday and summer weekend specials, most trains on the Glyn Valley Tramway were of the mixed variety. Here, Dennis waits at the head of a mixed train to Glyn Ceiriog at Chirk station on 30 May 1932.*

In 1861 a Bill was presented to Parliament for the building of the turnpike road and the tramway, but was thrown out by the House of Commons as they did not see it their duty to unite railways and roads! However, the road itself was built, partly funded by the Cambrian Slate Company, and opened in 1863 with adequate allowance in its width for the building of a tramway in the future.

Despite various other abortive plans to link the quarries at Glyn Ceiriog with the outside world it was only in 1870, with the passing of the Tramways Act by Parliament, that the building of the Glyn Valley Tramway became feasible. In 1871 the Shropshire Union Railway & Canal Company, owners of the Ellesmere Canal, were given sole rights to run the proposed tramway, in return for providing half of the capital required for its construction. The Glyn Valley Tramway Company was formed in March 1872, Henry Dennis was appointed engineer and construction started in June. The gauge selected for the

tramway was a curious 2ft 4¼in - apparently for no other reason other than it was exactly half the width of the British standard gauge of 4ft 8½in. The line opened for traffic in April 1873. Between Glyn Ceiriog and Pontfaen, where horse stables were located, the tramway ran alongside the road before crossing private land to the railway interchange sidings and the canal wharf south of Chirk. For the next 15 years, the tramway was operated by a team of up to eight horses. Wagons loaded with slate would travel by gravity down the valley as far as Pontfaen, where horse power would take over for the final steep climb to the railway and canal sidings. Empty wagons were hauled in the reverse direction by horse to Glyn Ceiriog. Passenger carrying cars were introduced in 1874, but were not a great success as they terminated at Pontfaen, which was nearly a mile away from Chirk GWR railway station. In 1875 a granite quarry opened at Hendre, three miles to the southwest of Glyn Ceiriog. Granite setts were in much demand at

Below *Built in 1917 by the Baldwin Locomotive Works of Philadelphia for use on narrow gauge lines in France during World War I, this 4-6-0 tank locomotive was introduced to the Glyn Valley Tramway in 1921.*

Right *Today, the Shropshire Union Canal is a popular route for holiday narrow boats. Here, north of Chirk station, the Glyn Valley Tramway once had an interchange wharf at Blackpark Canal Basin.*

CHIRK, PONTFADOG, and GLYNCEIRIOG.—Glyn Valley.

Sec. and Man., G. M. Jenkins, Chirk.

Miles	Up.	Week Days only.						
		mrn	aft	aft	aft	aft		
	Chirk ....dep.	10 0	1 40	3 25		3 40	6 10	
1¼	Pontfaen							
2	Castle Mill	b	b	b	b	b		
4	Pontfadog	10 11	1 51	3 36		3 51	6 19	
5	Dolywern	10 23	2 3	3 48		4 3	6 30	
6½	Glynceiriog ....arr.	10 40	2 20	3 56		4 11	6 38	
				4 5		4 20	6 45	

Miles	Down.	Week Days only.						
		mrn	mrn	non	aft	aft	aft	
	Glynceiriog ...dep.	7 40	11 15	12 0	2 25	4 40	6 50	
1¼	Dolywern	7 49	11 24	12 9	2 30	4 49	6 57	
2½	Pontfadog	7 57	11 32	12 17	2 41	4 57	7 5	
4½	Castle Mill	8 9	11 44	12 29	2 51	5 9	7 15	
5½	Pontfaen		b	b	b	b	b	
6½	Chirk 84, 87. arr.	8 20	11 55	12 40	3 0	5 20	7 25	

Except Weds. Weds. only. *Weds. only. Sats. only.* **b** Stops when required.

this time, with the construction of hundreds of street tramways in many of Britain's cities. Initially, the granite setts were carried by horse to the tramway railhead at Glyn Ceiriog for onward carriage to Chirk. However, this extra heavy traffic put more pressure on the horse drawn incline from Pontfaen to the railway and canal interchanges and, for the first time, serious thought was given to converting the line to steam traction, but it was not until 1885 with the passing of the Glyn Valley Tramway Act that this could become a reality. In the meantime, faced with increasing annual losses, the Shropshire Union Canal Company rid itself of the tramway, which was sold to the Glyn Valley Tramway Company in 1881.

The 1885 Act not only authorised the use of steam haulage but also allowed for the building of

Below Dennis *climbs up the 1888 route from Pontfaen and Chirk with a mixed train from Glyn Ceiriog on 31 May 1932.*

a new route into Chirk, thus bypassing the steep incline from Pontfaen, and an extension up the valley to Tregeiriog to serve the Hendre granite quarry. The new route and quarry extension were ready for traffic by 1888, and two steam locomotives were temporarily borrowed from the Snailbeach Railway to work trains. These were soon replaced by three new steam tram locomotives - *Sir Theodore* (named after the chairman of the GVT) and *Dennis* (named after the line's engineer) and *Glyn* - all built by Beyer Peacock of Manchester. The new extensions and the introduction of steam haulage transformed the fortunes of the railway, which was soon carrying increasing traffic not only to the new railway and canal interchanges at Chirk but also in the reverse direction up the valley. For the first time, new stations were built at Chirk and Glyn Ceiriog together with intermediate roadside waiting rooms at Pontfadog and Dolywern, and passenger trains started to run in 1891.

The new extension west of Glyn Ceiriog not

only served the granite quarry at Hendre but also other granite quarries at Teirw Hill and Upper Pandy, chinastone quarries at Cae Deicws and Lower Pandy and a silica quarry at Pen-y-Graig. During the summer, the little line was also well frequented by passengers wishing to explore the scenic delights of the Ceiriog Valley. During particularly busy times such as Bank Holidays, not only were all of the line's 14 passenger coaches pressed into service but also extra stone wagons fitted with crude seats were attached to the trains to cope with the extra customers.

During the early 20th century, the little line continued to prosper with increasing amounts of traffic, particulary granite, being carried down the

Right *Prior to the introduction of steam haulage and the opening of a new route between Pontfaen and Chirk in 1888, the horsedrawn GVT left the roadside at Pontfaen and crossed private land to canal and railway interchange wharves south of Chirk. The old route is now hidden in the treeline seen on the right.*

valley and general merchandise, such as coal, being carried up the valley. Passenger traffic, particularly during the summer, also showed growth. To cope with this increased traffic, a fourth engine was purchased in 1919. Built by the Baldwin Locomotive Works in the USA for use on military light railways in Europe during World War I, this 4-6-0 tank locomotive was converted to the Glyn Valley Tramway's gauge by Beyer Peacock and began work on the line in 1921.

Sadly, by the early 1930s the writing was on the wall for this delightfully idiosyncratic line. A downturn in the national economy led to a severe cutback in the use of granite for roadbuilding and, in 1932, a competing road bus service was introduced along the valley. This provided the death-knell for passenger traffic, which ceased to run on 6 April 1933. Freight traffic continued but, faced with increasing losses due to competion from lorries, the GVT's directors had no option

but to close the line completely. The last train ran on 6 July 1935. By 1936 the rails had been lifted, the locomotives were cut up for scrap, and wagons and carriages were either scrapped or sold off for other uses such as chicken sheds to local farmers. Fortunately, two original GVT coaches were saved and later found their way to the Talyllyn Railway. Thus ended the brief life of the Glyn Valley Tramway – or was it the end?

THE LINE TODAY

Despite the fact that the Glyn Valley Tramway closed over 73 years ago, there is still much to be discovered along the route of the line today. Starting at Chirk, descend to the towpath of the Shropshire Union Canal and follow it northwards for about one mile to the site of the Blackpark Canal basin. It was here that the GVT had a transshipment wharf with the canal. The route of the line southwards from here can be traced

Left *Named after the chairman of the GVT, Sir Theodore first began service on the tramway in 1888. Here he waits at Glyn Ceiriog with a lengthy passenger train for Chirk on 28 August 1926.*

Below *The route of the roadside tramway of the GVT between Pontfaen and Glyn Ceiriog is very easy to follow today. Here, on the B4500 between Pontfaen and Trout Hatchery, the wide grass verge speaks for itself!*

Above Dennis *pauses at Pontfadog with a mixed train for Glyn Ceiriog in May 1932. A loop was installed here to allow up and down trains to pass. As a result of competition from road buses, all passenger traffic ceased on the GVT less than a year later.*

through woodland adjoining the present main railway line. At Chirk, where the GVT had its own passenger station adjacent to the GWR mainline station (still open for business), the only overbridge on the route of the GVT can still be seen adjoining the main line overbridge.

Descending from Chirk along the B4500 we reach Pontfaen. Prior to 1888, the route of the GVT left the roadside here and wandered off across private land before climbing up to meet both the GWR railway interchange platform and then the Ellesmere Canal wharf. The 800yd incline was so steep (1 in 25) that slate and granite trains had be divided, so that the horses could cope with the heavy loads. This way of working was not at all satisfactory, and thus brought about both the diversion to Chirk and conversion to steam haulage. There are good views from Pontfaen of both the canal aqueduct, built in 1801 by Thomas Telford, and the later

railway viaduct, built in 1852, which both span the valley south of Chirk.

From Pontfaen to Glyn Ceiriog, the Glyn Valley Tramway was a true roadside tramway and today, when travelling up the valley, the wide roadside verge on the left of the road is a stark reminder of the line's route. After about three miles we enter the village of Pontfadog, where the GVT roadside waiting room, complete with sparse period character, original seats and fireplace, has been restored by the Glyn Valley Tramway Group and is open to the public.

Another mile takes us to the village of Dolywern where, in 1888, the line was re-routed on a girder bridge across the River Ceiriog to avoid a sharp bend in the road. The line rejoined its old roadside route on the other side of the village. Today, the girder bridge still exists and can be seen from the roadside on the eastern edge of the village. However, it is now in the grounds of a

Right *The waiting room at Pontfadog was on the opposite side of the road to the railway. The building has been bought by the Glyn Valley Tramway Group and its sparse interior with bare seats and fireplace is now open to the public.*

Leonard Cheshire home and necessary permission should be sought before inspecting the bridge. It is said that the roof of the cellar in the home is supported by old rails from the GVT!

Dolywern waiting room, complete with exterior clock, still exists but, again, it is within the boundary of the Cheshire Home. However, it can be clearly seen from the road.

Glyn Ceiriog, the terminus of GVT passenger trains, beckons just over a mile further west. Here, the former engine shed awaits restoration into a museum by the Glyn Valley Tramway Group. The station is now a private house, and there is a small museum devoted to the railway in the excellent Glyn Valley Hotel – during licensing hours! The GVT Group has also purchased a short section of trackbed on the site of the former coal wharf.

The Glyn Valley Tramway Group are planning to restore the former engine shed and yard in Glyn Ceiriog, where they will establish a museum and visitor centre. Future plans also include creating a short replica train. For more information about the GVT Group visit their website: www.glynvalleytramway.com

South of Glyn Ceiriog, the route of the 1888 extension can be followed between the Coed-y-Glyn granite quarry and Hendre Quarry. This section of the Glyn Valley Tramway was given to the National Trust in 1948 and is now a well-maintained footpath. Highlights of this walk are the girder bridge over the River Ceiriog at Upper Pandy and the remains of old quarry buildings hidden away in the undergrowth near Hendre Quarry.

Right *On the 1888 extension from Glyn Ceiriog to Hendre Quarry, the Glyn Valley Tramway crossed the River Ceiriog on this girder bridge near Upper Pandy Quarry. Following the route of the tramway as far as Hendre Quarry, this well-maintained footpath is now owned by the National Trust.*

Below *Glyn Ceiriog engine shed and station yard are currently owned by Wrexham County Borough Council. The Glyn Valley Tramway Group plan to establish a museum and visitor centre here, together with a short length of track and a short replica GVT train, in the future.*

Left *Hidden away in the undergrowth at the far end of the Hendre Quarry extension of the GVT, these former quarry buildings are now slowly being taken over by nature. The quarry at Hendre was worked between 1875 and 1950. Prior to the opening in 1888 of the GVT extension to the quarry, granite was carried by pack horse to the railhead at Glyn Ceiriog. Road transport took over after the line closed in 1935.*

Below *A quiet moment at Glyn Ceiriog in May 1932, with one of the tram locomotives running round a mixed train after arriving from Chirk. On the left is the engine shed which still stands today, and which the Glyn Valley Tramway Group eventually hope to turn into a museum.*

ORDNANCE SURVEY MAPS
Landranger 1:50,000 series Nos.125 & 126

TOURIST INFORMATION
Nearest offices: Oswestry Mile End Visitor Centre, Mile End Services, Oswestry, Shropshire, SY11 4JA (Tel. 01691 662488).
Oswestry Town Visitor Information Centre, Heritage Centre, 2 Church Terrace, Oswestry, Shropshire SY11 2TE (Tel. 01691 662753).

WHERE TO STAY
For accommodation in the Ceiriog Valley contact either of the Oswestry Tourist Information Centres (see above) or visit the Ceiriog Valley's Community Website: www.ceiriogvalley.org.uk

RAILWAY WALKS
Apart from the 1888 deviation at Dolywern where the GVT route now passes through the grounds of a Cheshire Home, it is still possible to follow the roadside section of the tramway on the verges of the B4500 between Pontfaen and Glyn Ceiriog.

South of Glyn Ceiriog a footpath, maintained by the National Trust, follows the route of the tramway between the Coed-y-Glyn Quarry and Hendre Quarry.

PLACES TO VISIT
- 13th century Chirk Castle (National Trust)
- Glyn Valley Tramway Museum at the Glyn Valley Hotel, Glyn Ceiriog
- Restored GVT waiting room at Pontfadog

WELSH HIGHLAND RAILWAY

CAERNARFON TO PORTHMADOG

For thousands of years, the mountains of northwest Wales have provided a natural barrier against foreign invaders. The Romans first penetrated the area in the 1st century AD and built a fort on the outskirts of what is now Caernarfon. Linked by a Roman road from Chester the fort, known as Segontium, was the most important in North Wales and held up to 1,000 infantry. Occupied for around 400 years, Segontium was located in a strategic position overlooking the Menai Straits.

However, it was Caernarfon itself, with its natural harbour and commanding position, that was chosen by Edward I in 1283 as the site for one of his mightiest castles during his campaign to subjugate the Welsh. In more modern times, Caernarfon Castle has been the venue for the investiture ceremony of the Prince of Wales and its importantance is recognised today with its status as a World Heritage site.

The surrounding mountains, collectively known as Snowdonia, had for centuries been quarried for their slate and mined for their minerals - such as copper, lead and silver - but the difficult terrain hampered progress and made transport difficult. Prior to the coming of railways in the early 19th century this was provided by horse-drawn sledges.

The first railways in the region were of a primitive type with various non-standard narrow gauges being used and operated as horse-drawn and gravity tramways. One of the first was the 3ft 6in gauge Nantlle Tramway which opened in 1828 to convey slate from quarries at Nantlle to

Left Overlooked by the summit of Snowdon, ex-South African Beyer-Garratt No. 138 Millennium coasts down from Rhyd-Ddu station with a train for Dinas and Caernarfon.

the harbour at Caernarfon. Other horse-drawn and gravity tramways soon followed - the 1ft 11½in gauge Ffestiniog Railway from Blaenau Ffestiniog to Porthmadog in 1836 and the 2ft gauge Croesor Tramway from Croesor to Porthmadog in 1864. By this date steam power was being introduced, and the Ffestiniog Railway became one of the first narrow gauge railways to take this important step in 1865.

Due to the difficult terrain of Snowdonia, standard gauge railways were much later on the scene - the coastal Bangor & Caernarvon Railway opened in 1854 and this was soon followed by the Carnarvonshire Railway from Caernarfon to Afon Wen and the Carnarvon & Llanberis Railway. In the south of the region, the standard gauge Aberystwyth & Welsh Coast Railway opened to Porthmadog and Pwllheli in 1869 and the Conwy Valley route from Llandudno Junction to Blaenau Ffestiniog in 1879.

Following the highly successful introduction of steam power and passenger services on the Ffestiniog Railway, the stage was now set for one of the most ambitious proposals for a narrow gauge railway network anywhere in Britain. The later formation of the Welsh Highland Railway had its roots in this complicated scheme.

HISTORY OF THE LINE
Proposed by the Ffestiniog Railway's chief engineer Charles Spooner, the North Wales Narrow Gauge Railways Company was an ambitious plan to link the towns, villages, quarries and mines of northwest Wales. Originally consisting of eight railways, the plan was finally watered down to just two - Croesor Junction to Bettws-y-Coed and Dinas (south of Caernarfon) to Bryngwyn (where Spooner owned a slate quarry), with a branch to Rhyd-Ddu. An Act of

Above *Oil-fired Beyer-Garratt No.138* Millennium *arrives at Caernarfon - the northern terminus of the Welsh Highland Railway. With a length of 48ft and weighing 62 tons this 2-6-2+2-6-2 locomotive is one of the most powerful of its type in the world.*

Parliament was obtained in 1872 and Charles Spooner was appointed Chief Engineer. The line to Bryngwyn was opened in 1877, and to Rhyd-Ddu in 1881 but the Croesor Junction to Bettws-y-Coed line was never built.

The NWNGR was never a financial success from the start. Losses mounted due to a recession in the slate industry, problems arose over transshipment costs with the London & North Western Railway at Dinas Junction, the company went into receivership and Charles Spooner relinquished his post as Chief Engineer. Despite all these problems, the NWNGR soldiered on and, in 1900, obtained a Light Railway Order to extend its line from Rhyd-Ddu to Beddgelert.

Meanwhile, yet another railway, the Portmadoc, Beddgelert & South Snowdon Railway, was formed in 1901. Under its incorporation under an Act of Parliament, the company was given powers to purchase the Croesor Tramway, also now in receivership, and to use it as part of its route to gain access to Rhyd-Ddu. The PB&SSR also had its eyes on the NWNGR and, with the purchase of this line in mind, obtained an Act of Parliament to build a line from Dinas Junction to Caernarfon Harbour - thus creating a through route between Porthmadog and Caernarfon. The extension to Caernarfon was never built, but work started on the section between Croesor Junction and Rhyd-Ddu. Although never completed, parts of this extension can still be seen today including a stone road bridge south of Beddgelert.

By the beginning of the 20th century and still in receivership, the NWNGR was facing a severe shortage of of reliable motive power. A replacement had to be found for worn-out Hunslet 0-6-4 tank locomotive *Beddgelert* but funds were not available. To protect its future purchase from complete closure, the PB&SSR stepped in and purchased 2-6-2 tank locomotive

Right *One of the major tourist attractions in the UK, Caernarfon Castle was built by Edward I during the 13th century in his bid to subjugate the Welsh. The WHR terminus is only a short walk from the castle.*

DINAS, BRYNGWYN, and SNOWDON.—North Wales Narrow Gauge.

Sec. and Man., G. C. Aitchison, 14, Dale Street, Liverpool.

Miles from Dinas.	Down.	Week Days only.		Miles	Up. Coaches leave	Week Days only.			
	471 BANGOR ....dep.				Beddgelert				
	471 CARNARVON ....''			3¼	Snowdon (Train) ....dep.				
	Dinas ....dep.			5¼	Quellyn Lake ....''				
2	Tryfan Junction ......arr.			7¼	Bettws Garmon				
—	Tryfan Junction ......dep.	SERVICE		9¼	Waenfawr				
2¼	Rhostryfan	SUSPENDED.		11	Tryfan Junction ......arr.				
4¼	Bryngwyn ....arr.			—	Mls Bryngwyn ....dep.				
—	Tryfan Junction ....dep.			—	1¼ Rhostryfan				
3¼	Waenfawr			—	2¼ Tryfan Junction ...arr.				
4¼	Bettws Garmon			—	Tryfan Junction ......dep.				
7¼	Quellyn Lake			13	Dinas 471 ....arr.				
9¼	Snowdon *			16¼	471 CARNARVON ......arr.				
13	Beddgelert † (Coach).. ''			25	471 BANGOR ....arr.				

* About 3 miles to the summit of Snowdon.　† 1½ miles from Pont Aberglaslyn; for Vale of Gwynant and Pass of Llanberis; Bettws-y-Coed; Portmadoc, &c.

Russell from Hunslet of Leeds in 1906 for use on the NWNGR. Despite this assistance from a separate railway company, the NWNGR's fortunes continued to decline and passenger traffic was suspended in 1916. Meanwhile, the painfully slow progress of the PB&SSR's extension from Croesor Junction to Rhyd-Ddu had come to a complete halt and the company had finally abandoned its grandiose scheme to link Porthmadog with Caernarfon. It still operated the horse-drawn Croesor Tramway, but the state of the track on that line was appalling. The outlook was bleak, and if it hadn't been for the intervention of Caernarvon County Council and other local authorities, the NWNGR would probably have completely closed by the early 1920s. The PB&SSR might have struggled on longer because of its minimal running and maintenance costs.

A public enquiry was held by the Light Railway Commissioners in 1921 and the outcome was the formation of the Welsh Highland Railway (Light Railway) Company in the following year. Financially backed by the Government and local authorities, the new company took over the NWNGR and the PB&SSR, including the latter company's scheme

to construct a railway linking Porthmadog with Caernarfon. The first section of the new Welsh Highland Railway to be reopened after remedial work to the track and rolling stock was the ex-NWNGR's route between Dinas Junction and South Snowdon, which opened to passengers in July 1922. This was followed in 1923 by the completion of the missing link between South Snowdon and Croesor Junction and relaying of track between there and Porthmadog. The extension to Caernarfon never materialised.

In the same year Colonel H. F. Stephens, the leading exponent of light railways in England and Wales, was appointed locomotive superintendent and civil engineer (and later Chairman) of the new railway - a timely appointment as the WHR was already facing a shortage crisis in its motive power and rolling stock departments.

Colonel Stephens overcame these problems by borrowing locomotives and passenger coaches from the Ffestiniog Railway. An ex-War Department Baldwin 4-6-0 tank locomotive and six new coaches were also purchased to cope with the predicted increase in tourist traffic. Sadly this never came and, coupled with a further decline in slate traffic, the WHR was soon struggling to survive. Despite being bailed out by the County

Right *A North Wales Narrow Gauge Railways train headed by 0-6-4 tank locomotive Moel Tryfan heads up the Vale of Bettws Garmon in the 1890s. Passengers on today's Welsh Highland Railway can also sit back and enjoy this beautiful scenery.*

Left *Dinas Junction on 31 August 1926. Even though the missing link between Rhyd-Ddu and Croesor Junction was completed in 1923, thus allowing through trains to run to Porthmadog, the original Welsh Highland Railway always struggled to survive. The modern-day WHR is also awaiting the completion of its missing link due in 2009.*

Below *Set amidst the majestic landscape of Snowdonia, Beyer-Garratt No. 138 Millennium departs from Rhyd-Ddu station with a train for Caernarfon. Rhyd-Ddu is the starting point for a strenuous walk to the summit of Snowdon, which can be seen towering in the distance.*

Above *A quiet moment at Beddgelert station in the 1930s. During the last years of operation, it was very rare for through trains to run between Porthmadog and Dinas Junction. Passengers wishing to travel further north or south were forced to change trains here.*

Council and the introduction of economies such as diesel traction, withdrawing winter passenger services and introducing a much-reduced summer timetable, it looked as if the line would close altogether in 1933. At the last minute, the WHR was saved when the Ffestiniog Railway agreed to lease it in 1934. The FR made great efforts to increase the popularity of the line, giving a new lick of colourful paint to stations and rolling stock, relaying track and introducing a Welsh hostess, dressed in national costume, at Beddgelert Station. Although the number of passenger trains was increased, very few ran the entire length of the line, thus necessitating a change and often lengthy wait at Beddgelert.

The Ffestiniog Railway experiment was shortlived and the last passenger train ran in September 1936. Goods trains continued to run but even these had ceased by the summer of 1937, and the Welsh Highland Railway gradually disappeared into the undergrowth. Track was

finally lifted between Dinas Junction and Croesor Junction in 1941, and the railway's rolling stock and locomotives were disposed of in 1942. Only one locomotive and some passenger carriages survived – *Russell* ended up working in an Oxfordshire quarry and the carriages became summer houses or garden sheds in local gardens. The track between Croesor Junction and Porthmadog was finally lifted after the war and, apart from a few intact bridges and abandoned station buildings, the Welsh Highland Railway had ceased to exist – but not forever!

THE LINE SINCE CLOSURE

Fortunately the trackbed of the Welsh Highland Railway, still in the hands of the Receiver, remained fairly undisturbed over the following years. The standard gauge railway from Caernarfon to Afon Wen closed in the 1960s and the trackbed converted to the Lon Eifion cycleway. At the same time, a group of enthusiasts

Right *The reopened WHR passes through some of the most dramatic scenery in Britain. This magnificent stretch of newly-laid track between Rhyd-Ddu and Beddgelert awaits the first scheduled Caernarfon to Porthmadog passenger train due at Easter 2009.*

SNOWDON MOUNTAIN RAILWAY

Operating on the Swiss Abt system, the 2ft 7½in gauge Snowdon Mountain Railway climbs from the low level terminus at Llanberis for 4½ miles on gradients as steep as 1 in 5.5 to the summit terminus at an altitude of 3,493ft above sea level. On its opening day on 6 April 1896, a train became derailed and a passenger was killed. After modifications to the rack rail and a reduction of the maximum load for locomotives, the line reopened on 9 April 1897. The line is currently operated by a mix of original Swiss-built 0-4-2 steam tank locomotives and more modern diesel counterparts

formed the Welsh Highland Light Railway (1964) Company with the long term aim of reopening the line. By the mid-1970s, this group of enthusiasts had purchased a strip of land adjacent to the Cambrian Coast standard gauge line at Porthmadog, laid a short stretch of 1ft 11½in gauge track as far as Pen-y-Mount and purchased Gelert's Farm for their base. Passenger trains first started running in 1980, but will cease in 2009 when the new main line opens to Porthmadog.

Meanwhile the only surviving WHR steam locomotive, *Russell*, had finished its working life at the Norden Clay Mines on the Isle of Purbeck in Dorset and was given to the Welsh Highland Light Railway Company by the Birmingham Locomotive Society in 1965. Following the fitting of a new boiler and total restoration at Gelert's Farm, *Russell* returned to service in 1987.

The story of the Welsh Highland Railway has never been straightforward and matters now took a further convoluted turn. In 1989 the Ffestiniog Railway became involved when they made a

Left Hunslet 2-6-2 tank locomotive Russell *and ex-War Department Baldwin 4-6-0 No.590 cross with their trains at Beddgelert in the 1930s.* Russell's *cab was cut down in 1924 to allow through running on the Ffestiniog Railway.*

Above *The missing link on the Welsh Highland Railway between South Snowdon and Croesor Junction was opened in 1923. Here Ffestiniog Railway 0-4-0* Little Giant *waits patiently by the brand-new water tower at Beddgelert station.*

secret bid to purchase the trackbed of the Welsh Highland Railway from the Official Receiver. Their long term aim was the reopening of the line between Caernarfon and Porthmadog where it would link up with their own system. This would create the longest narrow gauge journey anywhere in Britain – 40 miles from Caernarfon to Blaenau Ffestiniog. In 1993, the Ffestiniog Railway formed the Welsh Highland Railway Society to bring together volunteers to assist in the reopening of the line.

So it was that both the Welsh Highland Light Railway (1964) Company and the Ffestiniog Railway were now competing against each other to reopen the line. There then followed years of legal wrangling with a High Court hearing and several public inquiries, before the Ffestiniog Railway gained the necessary powers to purchase the trackbed from the Official Receiver. The guarantee of major funding for the reopening of the line was very important, and this was achieved through millions of pounds worth of grants from

Above *A hand-coloured postcard view of Aberglaslyn Pass in 1925. Here, the Baldwin 4-6-0 No.590 emerges from a tunnel with a northbound train from Porthmadog. The road on the opposite bank of the Afon Glaslyn is much wider and busier today.*

the Millennium Commission, European Regional Development Fund, the Welsh Assembly and the Wales Tourist Board. Once a Light Railway Order had been obtained, construction work started on the former standard gauge Caernarfon to Dinas section in 1997. Since then the line has been reopened in sections, first to Waunfawr in 2000, then to Rhyd-Ddu in 2003 and finally from Rhyd-Ddu to Portmadog via Beddgelert. Much of this section is now complete, including the installation of a new bridge over the Afon Glaslyn south of Beddgelert, the laying of track through the tunnels in Aberglaslyn Pass and a new bridge at Pont Croesor. At the southern end, new track has been laid from Pen-y-Mount to Traeth Mawr by the WHR (Porthmadog). Reopening of the final section to passengers, including a short distance through the streets of Porthmadog, is due for Easter 2009.

THE LINE TODAY

The reopened Welsh Highland Railway commences its journey at Caernarfon in the shadow of Edward I's famous castle. As far as Dinas the line uses the old trackbed of the standard gauge line to Afon Wen, which closed in the 1960s. A request halt is located at Bontnewydd. Most WHR trains include cycle wagons for cyclists using the Lon Eifion cycleway which parallels the line as far as Dinas. Here, the WHR has its permanent way department and locomotive and carriage sheds. From Dinas, the railway follows the trackbed of the original WHR as far as Rhyd-Ddu, with an intermediate station

Right inset *Another postcard view of the Aberglaslyn Pass taken from a photograph dated 1923. Here, Ffestiniog Railway 0-4-0 Prince heads out of a tunnel with a southbound train for Porthmadog.*

Right *The 300yd-long tunnel in Aberglaslyn Pass during reconstruction of the Welsh Highland Railway in 2007. Following closure of the line, the trackbed and tunnels through the Pass became a popular route for walkers. Steam trains will once more thunder through here in 2009.*

Welsh Highland Railway in Aberglaslyn Pass

WELSH HIGHLAND RAILWAY STATION, PORTMADOC.

at Waunfawr and request halts at Plas y Nant and Snowdon Ranger. Rhyd-Ddu is the jumping off point for walkers to the summit of Snowdon. Once the extension to Porthmadog is opened in 2009, the railway will pass through some of the most beautiful scenery in Britain - first skirting around the shores of Llyn Cwellyn on the western slopes of Snowdon before crossing the Afon Glaslyn south of Beddgelert and threading through rock-hewn tunnels along the Pass of Aberglaslyn.

Apart from its stunning scenery, the WHR also has another major attraction in its locomotives and passenger rolling stock. The railway possesses no fewer than five Beyer-Garratt articulated steam locomotives, which

Left *A postcard view of the Welsh Highland Railway station at Porthmadog - known as Portmadoc New, it was opened in 1923. The GWR Cambrian Coast line crossed the WHR on the level a short distance beyond the station.*

Below *By 1929 the Welsh Highland Railway was in a sorry state and economies were made such as relocating Portmadoc New station to the north of the GWR line. Here, the small tin waiting room waits forlornly for a few passengers.*

PORTMADOC
W. H. RLY.

are among the most powerful narrow gauge engines in the world. The oldest, the first of its type to be built, is an 0-4-0+0-4-0 that was delivered to the Tasmanian Government Railways in 1909. Four larger 2-6-2+2-6-2 locomotives, built between 1937 and 1958, were rescued from South Africa where they once operated on the Alfred County Railway. Once oil-fired, these 62 ton, 48ft-long, monsters are now being converted back to coal firing due to the spiralling cost of oil, and are capable of hauling 12 coach trains up

Below *Two gauges side-by-side at Porthmadog. Founded by a small group of enthusiasts in 1961, the Welsh Highland Railway (Porthmadog) was the first on the scene in the race to reopen the WHR.*

FFESTINIOG RAILWAY

Opened in 1836 as a horse-drawn and gravity tramway to carry slate from the quarries at Blaenau Ffestioniog down to the harbour at Porthmadog, the 1ft 11½in gauge Ffestiniog Railway was converted to steam power in 1865. Passenger services on this independent railway were withdrawn in 1939, but goods traffic continued through to 1946 when the line closed.

A preservation group was formed in 1951, and the first section of line from Porthmadog Harbour to Boston Lodge was reopened to passengers in 1955. The 13½-mile line was then reopened in stages to Tan-y-Bwlch, Ddualt, finally reaching Blaenau Ffestiniog in 1982.

Passengers are carried in Victorian rolling stock hauled by oil-fired steam locomotives, including the unique double Fairlies, all of which have been beautifully restored in the company's Boston Lodge Works.

Trains run on this scenic line throughout the year with a full service operating between the end of March and early November. From Easter 2009, the newly-opened Welsh Highland Railway will link up with the Ffestiniog Railway in Porthmadog and create a 40-mile long narrow gauge steam hauled route.

For more details about the Ffestiniog Railway visit their website: www.festrail.co.uk

Above and left *Pen y Mount station is on the short length of line currently open to passengers from Porthmadog to the newly-laid Traeth Mawr loop on the WHR main line. After years of acrimony, the Ffestiniog Railway and the Welsh Highland Railway (Porthmadog) seemed to have buried their differences*

1 in 40 gradients at a speed of 25 mph. No.138, built in 1958 by Beyer-Peacock of Manchester, has been named *Millennium*. A powerful diesel-hydraulic locomotive has also been purchased from South Africa, where it once operated at the Pretoria Portland Cement Company. This powerful 27-ton double-bogie locomotive, named *Castell Caernarfon*, is also used to haul passenger trains on the line.

The only surviving original WHR locomotive, *Russell*, has been restored by the WHR (Porthmadog) and is currently based at their Gelert Farm Works. It is hoped that this locomotive will one day return to its original stamping ground, hauling a set of vintage coaches.

The passenger rolling stock line-up also includes some museum pieces that have been rescued and restored by the WHR. These include the 1891 NWNGR 'Gladstone Car', the 1893 ex-NWNGR carriage that was converted to a buffet car by the original WHR in 1927 and an open toast rack coach that dates from 1924.

For more details about the Welsh Highland Railway visit their website: www.welshhighlandrailway.net

Right *The reopened WHR crosses the Cambrian Coast standard gauge line on this diamond crossing to the east of Porthmadog main line station.*

ORDNANCE SURVEY MAPS
Landranger 1:50,000 series Nos 115/124

TOURIST INFORMATION
Caernarfon: Caernarfon Tourist Information Centre, Oriel Pendeitsch, Stryd y Castell, Caernarfon LL55 2NA (tel. 01286 672232) or visit these websites: www.visitcaernarfon.com **or** www.caernarfon.com
Porthmadog: Porthmadog Tourist Information Centre, Stryd Fawr, Porthmadog LL49 9LD (tel. 01766 512981) or visit these websites: www.porthmadog.com **or** www.porthmadog.co.uk

WHERE TO STAY
There is a wide range of accommodation in Caernarfon, Porthmadog and in the Snowdonia National Park. For more details contact either Caernarfon or Porthmadog tourist information centres (see above).

RAILWAY WALKS
Now that the Welsh Highland Railway is reopening along its full length it is no longer possible to walk along the former trackbed. However, there are many walks, ranging from easy to hard, which can be made to and from stations along the line.
1. Caernarfon to Dinas along the Lon Eifion cycleway (Easy/2.5 miles)
2. Caernarfon to Waunfawr through the Gwyrfai Valley (Easy/5.5 miles)
3. Dinas to Bontnewydd via Rhostryfan and the Bryngwn branch trackbed (Easy/7 miles)
4. Waunfawr to Snowdon Ranger (Moderate/7 miles)
5. Snowdon Ranger to Rhyd-Ddu (Moderate/3 miles)
6. Snowdon Ranger to summit of Snowdon (Moderate/7 miles return)
7. Rhyd-Ddu to summit of Snowdon (Moderate/8 miles return)
8. Rhyd-Ddu to Nantlle Ridge circular (Hard/10 miles)

For more details of these walks visit: www.welshhighlandrailway.net/walks

PLACES TO VISIT
● Caernarfon Castle
● Segontium Roman Fort, Caernarfon
● Snowdon Mountain Railway
● Ffestiniog Railway
● Portmeirion

CORRIS RAILWAY

MACHYNLLETH - ABERLLEFENNI

Located at the lowest crossing point of the Afon Dyfi, Machynlleth is often referred to as the 'Ancient Capital of Wales'. Once an important centre for copper mining during the Bronze Age, the surrounding area was also occupied by the Romans who built a fort at Cefn Caer and lookout posts on nearby hills.

In 1291 the Lord of Powys was granted a charter by Edward I to hold a market in the town every Wednesday. The market was a great success and, by the 17th century, was drawing sellers and buyers of cattle from all over Wales and the English border counties. The market is still held today. Machynlleth was also the seat of Owain Glyndwr's Welsh Parliament after he was crowned Prince of Wales in the town in 1404, hence the town's claim to be the Ancient Capital.

The town has several ancient buildings including Royal House, so named after Charles I stayed here in 1643. Machynlleth's strategic importance grew further when a bridge was built over the Afon Dyfi in the early 16th century. However, due to increasing amounts of traffic, the bridge was replaced in 1805 by the present five-arched structure.

In 1644, Machynlleth was the scene of a bloody battle during the Civil War when Royalists occupying the town were routed by Cromwell's troops - many were killed and many buildings in the town were destroyed.

To the north, the Afon Dulas winds its way down from the hills before joining the Afon Dyfi a short distance from Machynlleth. In the valley, both Corris and neighbouring Aberllefenni had been important centres for the slate quarrying industry since the 16th century. For several hundred years the slate was carried by packhorse down the valley to boats on the Afon Dyfi.

However, increasing demand for the slate during the 19th century led to schemes for a horsedrawn tramway to carry the slate down the valley. In 1859, a 2ft 3in narrow gauge tramway was finally opened between Aberllefenni and Derwenlas on the Afon Dyfi, southwest of Machynlleth. This tramway predated the standard gauge Newtown & Machynlleth Railway which was opened in 1861. A further extension of the latter line was opened by the Aberystwyth & Welsh Coast Railway to Aberystwyth in 1863. Both railways were merged to form the Cambrian Railways in 1864, and the section of the horsedrawn tramway between Machynlleth and Derwenlas was closed.

Left *Erected about 150 years ago, these sturdy slate and wire fences have stood the test of time and clearly mark the route of the Corris Railway between Corris and Garneddwen.*

Above *A typical Corris Railway mixed train prior to the takeover of the railway by the Great western railway in 1930. The Hughes 0-4-0 saddle tank locomotives were introduced in 1879.*

Above *Rebuilt in 1904, Machynlleth Station still stands today and is now a private residence. Also still extant, the corrugated iron shed to the left was once used to garage the railway's motor buses.*

HISTORY OF THE RAILWAY

In 1864, an Act of Parliament was passed permitting the use of locomotives on the section of tramway between Machynlleth and Aberllefenni and the old Corris, Machynlleth & River Dovey Tramroad changed its name to the Corris Railway Company.

Although the use of locomotives was now permitted, the Corris Railway continued to use horse power until 1879. In the intervening years, transshipment wharves came into use at Machynlleth so that slate could be transferred directly to Cambrian Railways wagons. The Corris was taken over in 1878 by Imperial Tramways of Bristol and J R Dix became General Manager. A forward-thinking man, Dix introduced steam locomotives and small passenger carriages to the line in 1879. However, the passenger carriages were still hauled by horses and this service was soon withdrawn due to complaints by quarry owners that it delayed their slate shipments.

In the end, an Act of Parliament was passed in 1883 allowing steam hauled passenger services to run between Machynlleth and Corris. This service was later extended to Aberllefenni in 1887. The Corris Railway flourished under Dix's management and was profitable until the early years of the 20th century. Towards the end of his tenure, Machynlleth station was rebuilt and a new steel bridge was erected over the Afon Dyfi.

The decline of the Corris started with the closure of two slate quarries in Upper Corris in 1904 and 1906, followed by the departure of J R Dix as manager in 1907. Faced with a declining slate industry, the little railway's new manager, J J O'Sullivan, actively promoted the tourist potential of the line. The most successful venture was the circular tour that involved using the Cambrian Railways main line between Machynlleth and Towyn, the Talyllyn Railway between Towyn and Abergynolwyn, a connecting bus service (using the Corris railway's own buses) between Abergynolwyn and Corris and the final link in the circle from Corris to Machynlleth on the Corris Railway. These proved extremely popular during summer months, especially after the

introduction of motor buses in 1908.

Very heavily dependent on the see-saw fortunes of the slate industry, slate tonnages held up reasonably well and were joined by new traffic in locally grown timber during World War I. Even after the war, the line was kept fairly busy not only with outgoing timber and slate but also with incoming coal and general merchandise. By the early 1920s slate production actually saw an increase but, by now, the three steam locomotives purchased from the Hughes Locomotive Company in 1878 were showing their age. A new locomotive was now needed to cope with the traffic but, as the Hughes Company no longer existed, the Corris bought an 0-4-2 saddle tank from the Kerr Stuart Company. This was delivered in 1921 and was always known as No. 4.

Omitted from the Railway Grouping of 1923, the Corris Railway continued on its independent way until 1928

Right *Built on the site of the old Corris Railway bridge and opened in 2000, the appropriately named Millennium Bridge now only carries cyclists and pedestrians across the Afon Dyfi. The bridge forms part of Route 8 of the National Cycle Network.*

when events in far off Bristol were soon to have a devastating impact on the line's future. The major shareholder of the Bristol Tramways Company (owner of the Corris), Sir George White, had died and his interests, mainly buses and trams, were sold to the Great Western Railway. Thus the GWR gained control of the Corris Railway in 1930. They had no idea what they had bought and showed a singular lack of interest in its purchase apart from the fleet of buses then being run by the Corris. The damage was done and by the end of 1930 passenger services were withdrawn, the buses sold off, and railway staff reduced to a minimum.

Amazingly, the Corris Railway survived for another 17 years. In that period it became a shadow of its former self, with usually only one steam engine in operation to haul what was left of the declining slate traffic along poorly maintained and overgrown track.

Beyond all odds the Corris

Above *The first railway bridge over the Afon Dyfi was built of timber but was replaced by this more substantial steel girder structure in 1908. Here a typical Corris Railway passenger train trundles across the bridge on its journey up the Dulas Valley to Corris. The small goods truck at the rear appears to have two extra passengers!*

ABERLLEFENI, CORRIS, and MACHYNLLETH.—Corris.
Gen. Man., D. J. McCourt, Machynlleth; Sec., F. H. Withers, Machynlleth.

Week Days only.

Miles		mrn	mrn	aft	aft	aft	6A15	7 37
	Aberllefeni .... dep.	7B30	9 50	1230	4 30	...	6A15	7 37
¼	Garneddwen	a	a	a	a		a	a
1½	Corris ‖ .... { arr.	7 38	9 58	1238	4 38	6F 5		
	.... { dep.	7 45	10 0	1245	4 42	6F12	...	
2	Esgairgeiliog	7 52	10 7	1252	4 53	6F19	...	
4	Llwyngwern	7 59	10 14	1258	5 1	6F30	...	
6	Ffridd Gate ‡	583	a	a	a	a		
6½	Machynlleth 578, 585, arr.	8B10	1025	1 10	5 15	6F30	...	

Week Days only.

Miles		mrn	mrn	aft	aft	aft	Fris. and Sats.	aft
	Machynlleth .... dep.	9B5	11 25	2 0	5 35	...		7 0
	Ffridd Gate ‡	a	a	a	a			7 12
2¼	Llwyngwern	9B17	11 37	2 12	5 47			7 18
3½	Esgairgeiliog	9B23	11 43	2 18	5 53			7 25
5	Corris ‖ .... { arr.	9B30	11 50	2 30	6 0			7 27
	.... { dep.	9 32	11 52	2 32	6A2			7 27
6	Garneddwen	a	a	a	a	6A10		
6½	Aberllefeni .... arr.	9 38	12 0	2 38	6A10			7 35

a Stops when required.
B Mondays only.
A Runs on 1st Wednesday and 2nd Monday in each month.
F Fridays and Saturdays.
‡ Station for Llanwrin.
‖ Station for Cader Idris (3½ miles) and Tal-y-llyn Lake (3 miles).

Railway became part of the nationalised British Railways on 1 January 1948. By now there was only one engine operational on the Corris, and the line was in a sorry state. Furthermore, no action was being taken to stop the erosion of the railway's embankment by the frequent flooding of the Afon Dyfi. The end finally came during a weekend in August when the Dyfi once again burst its banks and rendered most of the line inaccessible from Machynlleth. The line could well have been saved and may have then made it for a few more years into the preservation era of the 1950s. Sadly, total indifference from its new masters at the newly formed British Railways was the final nail in the railway's coffin.

A short distance over the mountains, the Talyllyn Railway was still struggling on under the ownership of Sir Haydn Jones. On his death in 1950 it seemed certain that the line would close but, fortunately, a group of railway enthusiasts stepped in to save the line and formed the Talyllyn Railway Preservation Society. Most of their locomotives and rolling stock were in a run-down state and they had to look further afield before they could reopen the line for the 1951

Below *Esgairgeiliog Station before the withdrawal of passenger services on the Corris Railway in 1930. A steeply graded branch, carried on a bridge over the Dulas, once led down to two slate quarries here. The quarry branch was abandoned in the late 1920s.*

Above *Esgairgeiliog Station is now preserved and serves as a bus shelter. Reached by a steep path from the village down in the valley, the station may yet witness steam trains again in the future, if the Corris Railway Society have their way!*

summer season. After negotiating with British Railways (Western Region), the Society was able to purchase some redundant Corris Railway equipment that was stored in the yard at Machynlleth, including locomotives Nos 3 and 4, some rolling stock and a quantity of rail, all for a knockdown price. The two locomotives and rolling stock were refurbished and became the mainstay of operations on the Talyllyn. They are still working on the line today.

The bridge over the Afon Dyfi was demolished soon after closure of the Corris and, apart from a few station buildings that remained intact, within a few years the little railway had disappeared into the undergrowth of the Dulas Valley.

THE LINE TODAY

It now seems to be a common theme in Britain for long-closed narrow gauge railways to rise from the ashes many years after closure. The Corris Railway is no exception to this rule! Formed in 1966 with the plan of eventually reopening the line, the Corris Railway Society was immediately faced with many seemingly insurmountable problems. All of the track had long been lifted, Corris and Aberllefenni stations had been demolished, the two surviving

Above and left *Recently introduced to haul passenger trains between Corris and Maespoeth, 0-4-2 saddle tank No. 7 was built from scratch by members of the Corris Railway Society. The design is based on that of Kerr Stuart No. 4 which was delivered new to the Corris Railway in 1921. The latter was purchased for £25 by the Talyllyn Railway in 1951 and is still in use on that line. Here, No. 7 waits for water at the restored Maespoeth engine shed before hauling its train back to Corris.*

FFRIDD WOOD, CORRIS RAILWAY 938

locomotives and much rolling stock had gone to their new home on the neighbouring Talyllyn Railway, the bridge over the Dyfi had been demolished and, although intact, the engine shed at Maespoeth was now owned by the Forestry Commission.

Progress was slow but, by 1970, the Society had purchased the former stables at Corris where they subsequently opened a museum. The breakthrough came in 1981 when Maespoeth engine shed was purchased from the Forestry Commission. Since restored, it is now the Society's headquarters. Five diesel locomotives were purchased and tracklaying between Corris and Maespoeth began in the 1980s. The first train since closure ran in 1985 and, since then, both of the original Corris locomotives bought by the Talyllyn have revisited their old line. Regular passenger services commenced between Corris and Maespoeth in 2002. These are are now hauled by 0-4-2 saddle tank locomotive No. 7, which

Left *Presently the end of the line from Corris, Maespoeth was once the junction for a tramway serving four slate quarries in Upper Corris. The short length of line in the foreground is all that remains of the tramway.*

Above *A Corris Railway passenger train tackles the gradient through Ffridd Wood on its journey up the valley to Corris. The closeness of the slate retaining wall on the road side of the line meant that passenger carriages only had doors on one side.*

was built by the Society and based on the original Corris Railway No. 4 purchased from Kerr Stuart in 1921. The Society's future plans include an extension of the line south of Maespoeth to Tan-y-Coed. However, there are many obstacles to overcome if the Corris is ever to steam into Machynlleth again.

For more details of the Corris Railway Society contact them at Corris Railway Museum, Station Yard, Corris, Machynlleth, Powys SY20 9SH or visit their website: www.corris.co.uk

Apart from the short stretch of reopened line between Corris and Maespoeth, much of the route of the old Corris Railway can still be traced today. Starting at Machynlleth, the former Corris station building is now a private residence and the station yard is a recycling point. The old corrugated iron shed next to the station building was once used as a garage for the Corris

Above *Final days on the Corris Railway. Introduced in 1878, No. 3 steams slowly along overgrown track at the long closed station of Aberllefenni with a short train of empty slate wagons. No. 3 has operated as* Sir Haydn *on the Talyllyn Railway since 1951.*

Railway's buses. To remind us of the past, the Corris Railway Society have preserved a pair of original 2ft 3in points in ballast alongside the adjoining main road.

Northeast of Machynlleth, the railway bridge over the Afon Dyfi has long since gone and was replaced in 2000 by a very modern structure appropriately named Millennium Bridge. On the route of the National Cycle Route No. 8, the bridge is part of the National Cycle Network and allows both pedestrians and cyclists to safely cross the Dyfi. Sadly, the designers of the bridge did not have the foresight to make allowances for the possible reopening of the Corris Railway sometime in the future.

The route of the line can be followed up the winding Dulas Valley as it runs parallel to the A487. Stopping or parking along this road to Corris is not recommended – or even allowed in many places! The alternative is to follow the unclassified road that starts at Glanfechan and runs along the eastern banks of the Dulas past the Centre for Alternative Technology, through Esgairgeiliog and on to Corris. North of Pantperthog, the former Corris station at Llwyngwern still exists and can be reached along a section of trackbed that is now a footpath. The Centre for Alternative Technology now occupies the site of a former slate quarry which was once served by the Corris Railway. North of the CAT is the Forestry Commission's picnic site, car park and forest trails at Tan-y-Coed. The Corris Railway Society hope to locate their southern terminus near here in the future.

High above the river and the village it served, the roadside station building at Esgairgeiliog has been beautifully preserved. It is not possible to stop on the A487 at this point, but the station can be reached from the village on a steep footpath. The steepest section of the Corris Railway lies

Right *The delightful setting of the Corris Railway as it wends its way up the Dulas Valley is much in evidence on this newly-opened section of line between Maespoeth and Corris. Train services operate on most weekends between April and September.*

TALYLLYN RAILWAY

A near neighbour of the Corris Railway, the Talyllyn Railway opened in 1865 to carry slate from the Bryn Eglws quarries to the harbour at Towyn. In 1951, this 7-mile-long, 2ft 3in narrow gauge railway became the first in the world to be saved from closure and preserved. The railway was bought in 1911 by the local MP, Sir Haydn Jones, who also developed the tourist potential of the line. Following closure of the quarries in 1946, the little line struggled on with passenger trains only running in the summer months. Sir Haydn died in 1950 and a group of preservationists took over the railway. The purchase of two locomotives, rolling stock and track from the recently-closed Corris Railway was a major contributor to the revitalisation and future success of the Talyllyn.

Above *Hauled by ageing locomotive No. 3, a slate train heavily loaded with cut slabs from the quarries at Aberllefenni steams slowly into Corris during the last few years of operation.*

Right inset *One of the original Hughes 0-4-0 saddle tanks pauses at the covered station at Corris with a short up freight. The station buildings were demolished in 1968 to make way for a car park.*

north of Esgairgeiliog and it was here that heavily laden trains would often stall. To aid progress, the fireman would sit on the locomotive's front buffer beam and liberally sprinkle sand on the rails.

Adjacent to the A487 one mile south of Corris, the engine shed and yard at Maespoeth are only accessible to the public by train from Corris. Maespoeth was once the junction for the tramway to the slate quarries at Upper Corris and a short section of this line is still used by the Society as a siding today. At Corris the delightful covered station was demolished in 1968, but the former stables are now the location for the Corris Railway Museum. The small car park here also serves the local doctor's surgery, which is in an adjacent Portakabin!

Beyond Corris Station the line crossed the

river on a stone arched bridge. This can still be seen today by taking a walk along the main street of the village where the railway once wound its way between the village houses. Beyond Corris, the route of the line up the Dulas Valley to Aberllefenni is easily followed from the roadside. In the valley beyond Corris the trackbed is clearly visible, with the original slate fencing still marking its route across the fields. At Garneddwen the railway once crossed the road here on a level crossing, and its trackbed is now the road to a terrace of former quarry workers' houses. In front

Right *Hemmed in by slate walls, recently-built 0-4-2 saddle tank No. 7 slowly departs from Corris with a train for Maespoeth. The building behind the train now houses the Corris Railway Museum.*

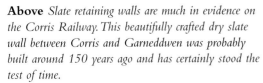

Above *Slate retaining walls are much in evidence on the Corris Railway. This beautifully crafted dry slate wall between Corris and Garneddwen was probably built around 150 years ago and has certainly stood the test of time.*

Left *Slate and wire fences are also still much in evidence along the route of the Corris Railway. The fencing is not only used to protect the trackbed of the railway, seen here on the northeastern edge of Corris, but also fields and a cemetery.*

Right *Victorian craftsmanship in all its glory can still be seen today between Garneddwen and Aberllefenni. Topped by a cast iron railing, these slate steps allowed access to the Corris Railway which once passed above the road on this dry slate retaining wall.*

Left *The horse-drawn tramway from Aberllefenni to Hengae Quarry also served this slate cutting shed. Although the tramway has long gone, the sheds are still being used for their original purpose.*

Below *Slate, slate everywhere. Most of the slate quarries around Aberllefeni are now silent, but the ghosts of their industrious past - spoil heaps, inclines, winding gear and houses - are littered everywhere around the barren landscape.*

of the houses a beautifully built dry slate retaining wall still survives, complete with original slate steps and cast iron hand rails. Aberllefenni station has long been demolished and its site is now occupied by council houses.

Aberllefenni was the end of the line for steam haulage and passenger services. Beyond here, the railway continued as two separate horse-drawn tramways to Ratgoed Quarry and Aberllefenni Quarry at Hengae. Much of the route of the former can still be seen today, and part of the trackbed is now a Forestry Commission track.

Several important buildings still remain intact at Aberllefenni including the slate cutting sheds, which are still in use, and the quarry workers' wages office which still carries its old bell on the roof. The extensive quarry at Hengae is now silent but all around are massive spoil heaps, inclines and winding gear. The former quarry manager's office here is now used as a small factory producing handmade paper from sheep's wool! Amazingly, at the foot of the incline behind the office there is still a short stretch of 2ft 3in track amidst all of the dereliction. It is now hard to imagine how busy this scene was during the heyday of the slate industry over 100 years ago.

ORDNANCE SURVEY MAPS
Landranger 1:50,000 series Nos 124 & 135

TOURIST INFORMATION
Machynlleth: Machynlleth Tourist Information Centre, Royal House, Penrallt Street, Machynlleth, Powys SY20 8AG (tel. 01654 702401) **or** Mid-Wales Tourism, The Station, Machynlleth, Powys SY20 8TG (tel. 01654 702653). Website: visitmidwales.co.uk
Corris: Corris Tourist Information Centre, Corris Craft Centre, Corris, Powys SY20 9SP (tel. 01654 761244)

WHERE TO STAY
There is a wide range of accommodation in the Machynlleth and Corris area. For more details contact the local tourist information centres (see above).

RAILWAY WALKS
Although much of the route of the Corris Railway can be easily traced from adjacent roads, there are few footpaths of any length on the trackbed itself. Short sections that can be walked include the route just north of the new Millennium Bridge over the Afon Dyfi. A short section from just north of Pantperthog to Llwyngwern near the Centre for Alternative Technolgy is also a footpath. Although not actually on the trackbed, a walk along the road between Corris Station and Aberllefenni is very rewarding with good views of the slate-fenced trackbed much in evidence. Part of the horse-drawn tramway between Aberllefenni and Ratgoed Quarry is now a Forestry Comission track and public footpath.

PLACES TO VISIT
- Royal House, Machynlleth
- Parliament House, Machynlleth
- Wednesday Market, Machynlleth
- Millennium Bridge over Afon Dyfi
- Centre for Alternative Technology
- Esgairgeiliog Station
- Corris Railway Museum
- Corris Craft Centre, Braichgoch
- King Arthur's Labyrinth, Braichgoch

Above *This short stretch of 2ft 3in gauge tramway track still exists below an incline at the Hengae Quarry, near Aberllefenni. It once carried loaded slate wagons from a lower adit.*

Right *The end of the line at Aberllefenni shortly after closure. It was not long before nature started taking over again. The Corris Railway Society has no plans to reopen this section of line from Corris.*

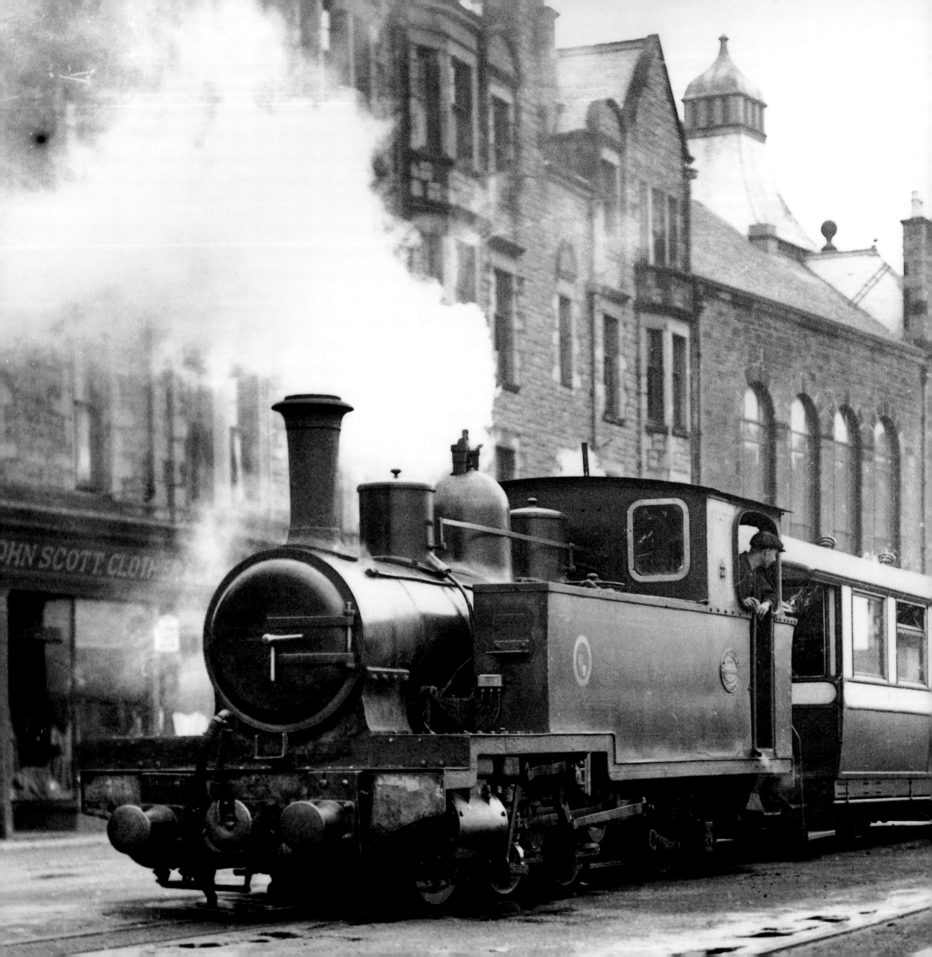

CAMPBELTOWN & MACHRIHANISH LIGHT RAILWAY

CAMPBELTOWN TO MACHRIHANISH

Sandwiched between the Atlantic Ocean and the Firth of Clyde and bathed by the mild Gulf Stream, the 45-mile Kintyre Peninsula is a narrow strip of land on Scotland's west coast. Connected to the Scottish mainland by a narrow isthmus at Tarbert, the peninsula is mountainous apart from a low-lying plain in the far south. Here, the town of Campbeltown, with its sheltered natural harbour, was once a prosperous fishing port and centre for shipping, boat building and whisky distilling.

Founded in the early 17th century, Campbeltown had become a Royal Burgh by 1800 and was soon attracting wealthy Glasgow businessmen who were responsible for much of the substantial architecture that can be seen in the town today.

Between 1880 and the 1920s there were 34 distilleries, producing 2 million gallons of whisky each year. Not surprisingly, Campbeltown proclaimed itself the 'whisky capital of the world'.

On the opposite side of the peninsula, coal had been mined around the coastal village of Machrihanish since the late 15th century. By the late 18th century, the growth of the local whisky industry had led to increased demand for the coal and, in 1773, James Watt was commissioned to survey a canal to link the collieries with Campbeltown. The 3-mile-long Campbeltown and Machrihanish Canal was opened in 1794 but by the mid-19th century it had fallen into disuse. The main colliery near Machrihanish was purchased in 1875 by the Argyll Coal & Canal Company, who also planned to replace the disused canal by a light industrial tramway.

Right *Now boarded up, this stone arch was once used by train passengers at Machrihanish to enter the grounds of the Ugadale Arms Hotel.*

Left *Built by Andrew Barclay of Kilmarnock, 0-6-2 tank locomotive* Atlantic *waits at the Hall Street terminus in Campbeltown with the 1.10pm 'Steamer Express' for Machrihanish on 2 August 1930.*

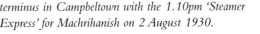

HISTORY OF THE LINE

Although the Argyll Coal & Canal Company had originally intended to follow the line of the disused canal for the route of their new tramway, in practice this did not happen. Construction work on the lightly laid 4¼-mile, 2ft 3in gauge, line from the mine at Kilkivan to Campbeltown started in 1876 and was completed by May 1877. Motive power was initially supplied by an 0-4-0 tank engine, subsequently named *Pioneer*, that had been ordered from Andrew Barclay of Kilmarnock.

By 1881 the railway was extended to a new colliery at Drumlemble and, within a few years, coal traffic on the line had become so heavy that the company ordered a second locomotive, named *Chevalier*, from Andrew Barclay.

In 1897, the Argyll Coal & Canal Company was taken over by the Campbeltown Coal Company. The line continued to flourish and a third locomotive, *Princess*, was ordered from Kerr Stuart to cope with the heavy traffic.

The early years of the 20th century also saw the beginningss of a new tourist trade to this part of Kintyre. The introduction of fast turbine steamers by Denny's of Dumbarton between Glasgow and Campbeltown saw thousands of day trippers descending on the town during the summer. Many of them were then conveyed six miles across to the seaside village of Machrihanish by horse-drawn carriage, where they could enjoy the beaches, golf links and bracing sea air.

Trade became so brisk that a new company, the Argyll Railway Company, was formed to take over the existing coal tramway and reopen and

Hall Street, Campbeltown.

Above and left: *Hall Street terminus in Campbeltown then and now. The postcard view shows one of the Andrew Barclay 0-6-2 tanks waiting with a three coach train before departing on its slow and ponderous journey to Machrihanish. Trains were timed to take 30 minutes for the 6 mile journey - an average speed of 12 mph!*

Apart from the cars, the modern view shows how little the scene has changed today. A grassed central reservation with bollards, flower beds and a palm tree has replaced the railway track and, in the distance, the Royal Hotel is still open for business.

become known, ordered a new 0-6-2 tank locomotive from Andrew Barclay. Delivered in June 1906 and named *Atlantic,* it soon proved its worth and a second locomotive, *Argyll,* was ordered in 1907. To cope with the forecast heavy passenger traffic, six bogie carriages were also delivered in 1906. There were no major engineering works on the line apart from the cutting between Limecraigs, where the railway had its sidings and sheds, and Campbeltown Harbour. Apart from a small shelter at Machrihanish, there were no station buildings, and the intervening halts were request stops at level crossings.

Without any fanfare or ceremony, the new railway finally opened in August 1906, nearly eight months later than planned. Until the outbreak of World War I, passenger traffic from the Clyde steamers was brisk enough during the summer months to warrant up to eight trains each day. At other times this reduced to three a day, with none on Sundays.

World War I saw the ending of the Clyde

Above and right *The only major engineering work on the Campbeltown & Machrihanish Light Railway was the excavation of a long cutting that took the line from the shore of Campbeltown Loch up to the summit of the line at Limecraigs. It was here that the railway had its engine and carriage sheds, coal depot and sidings. Today, the cutting is a well-surfaced cycleway and footpath complete with street lighting.*

extend it as a passenger-carrying line between the harbour at Campbeltown and Machrihanish Golf Links. The company applied for a Light Railway Order in 1904 and approval for the construction of the 6½-mile line was given in May 1905.

As with other proposed British light railways of this time, the promoters of the new line were totally over optimistic with their forecasts for future passenger and freight traffic. In particular, they forecast continuing growth in coal production whereas, if the truth had been known, the reserves of coal at the Argyll Colliery were nearly exhausted.

Construction work on the new line started immediately and the Campbeltown & Machrihanish Light Railway Company, as it had steamer services and train services on the railway were much reduced. Following the cessation of hostilities in 1918, the steamer traffic resumed and during the summer the passenger trains were bursting again with daytrippers. By the early 1920s, however, several factors spelled the beginning of the end for the line. Coal output from the Argyll Colliery was dwindling and competition from rival motor buses was increasing. The closure of the colliery in 1929 was the final nail in the coffin for the Campbeltown & Machrihanish and the line closed in November 1931. It was briefly reopened for traffic in January 1932, but by May it had closed again - this time for good. The company was wound up in 1933 and the track lifted the following year. Both of the remaining 0-6-2 tank locomotives, *Atlantic* and *Argyll,* were scrapped but the passenger carriages, minus bogies, found a new use in Campbeltown as holiday homes and, during World War II, as store sheds for the Admiralty.

THE LINE TODAY

The terminus of the Campbeltown & Machrihanish Light Railway in Campbeltown was alongside the once bustling harbour in Hall Street, just in front of the Royal Hotel. Apart from a small railway office there were no station buildings, and the single track and run-round loop were set into the road surface. Although the harbour is now quiet and the Clyde steamers have long since gone, the Royal Hotel is still there and the scene in Hall Street today is much the same, albeit with more road traffic and traffic islands. At the southern end of Hall Street, the route of the railway can be easily followed along the shore of Campbeltown Loch until it makes a sharp turn to the west through a long cutting before emerging at its summit at Limecraigs. Here, 100ft above sea level, the railway company had its locomotive and carriage sheds, coal depot and sidings.

Today, the long cutting from the harbour to Limecraigs is easily followed and is now a tarmacked cyclepath and footpath complete with

Left *Viewed from the balcony end of Coach No.5,* Atlantic *trundles bunker first across the flat South Kintyre landscape with a train for Machrihanish in August 1930 - only 18 months before closure.*

Left *The trackbed of the railway has long since disappeared beneath ploughed fields as this modern view taken near the site of Machrihanish Farm Halt clearly shows. A branch serving the Argyll Colliery left the main line at this point. The closure of the colliery in 1929 and competition from motor buses brought about the early demise of the line.*

Right *Atlantic forlornly waits for passengers at the Machrihanish terminus before departing on the 2.15pm train for Campbeltown in August 1930. A bleak place with only a rudimentary shelter, the terminus was located behind the imposing Ugadale Arms Hotel. Still standing, the hotel has recently been converted into luxury flats.*

Below *Machrihanish today. The terminus of the Campbeltown & Machrihanish lay immediately behind the Ugadale Arms Hotel which can be seen in a semi-derelict state in the middle distance. Although houses have since been built behind the hotel, the views of the Atlantic Ocean and the Links haven't changed.*

Above *Once the premier hotel in Machrihanish, the Ugadale Arms is now being converted into luxury flats. Railway passengers alighted at the terminus behind the hotel and found their way through this stone archway.*

street lighting. Nothing now remains of the Limecraigs sheds or trackbed, as much of this part of Campbeltown has been developed with new housing and playing fields. Following the level route of the line towards Machrihanish is also quite difficult, as the lightly laid trackbed has disappeared beneath ploughed fields.

However, it is possible to get some idea of the terrain that the railway crossed by taking the unclassified road to Campbeltown Airport, via the B842 and B843 towards Machrihanish. Here, south of the bridge over Machrihanish Water, part of which was the former canal bed, the railway crossed the road on the level. At this point there are ploughed fields to east and west, so completely has the trackbed disappeared. Another location to savour this disappearing act is at West Machrihanish, where the railway ran close to the canal before branching off to the long-closed Argyll Colliery.

Machrihanish is soon reached and its attraction to the promotors of the Campbeltown & Machrihanish Light Railway is obvious. To the north, pounded by Atlantic waves, the Links of Machrihanish stretch for over three miles and were a favourite spot for visitors in the summer. Adjoining The Links is the world-famous Machrihanish Golf Club which extends for 6,000yds along the shore. The 18-hole course has been voted to have 'the best opening hole in golf' anywhere in the world. Apart from these two major attractions, Machrihanish is also home to a major RAF base which boasts one of the longest runways in Europe. The airbase is currently mothballed on a 'care and maintenance' basis but the small civil airport still functions with its daily flight to and from Glasgow.

The only tangible link to the old railway still left in Machrihanish is the former Ugadale Arms Hotel, behind which lies the site of the line's terminus. Here, the route of the railway can be easily traced behind the hotel and for a short distance as it runs behind gardens towards Campbeltown. The red sandstone arch through which passengers from the railway entered the hotel gardens is still perfectly intact although the doorway is now boarded over. By far the largest building in the village, the hotel is now being converted into luxury flats.

As a coal-carrying tramway in the late 19th century the railway was a success. On its opening as a passenger line in 1906, the Campbeltown & Machrihanish Railway was the most isolated in Britain and, mainly due to its promoter's wildly over-optimistic forecasts over passenger numbers, never lived up to expectations. Sadly, today, very little remains of this Edwardian narrow gauge railway adventure.

ORDNANCE SURVEY MAP
Landranger 1:50,000 series No. 68

TOURIST INFORMATION
Campbeltown Tourist Information Centre, MacKinnon House, The Pier, Campbeltown, Kintyre, Strathclyde PA28 6EF (tel. 08452 255121)

WHERE TO STAY
There is limited accommodation in Campbeltown and Machrihanish. For more information contact Campbeltown Tourist Information Centre (see above)

RAILWAY WALKS
Although much of the trackbed has long disappeared beneath ploughed fields it is still possible to follow the route of the railway from its former terminus in Hall Street, Campbeltown, along the shore of the loch and up through the cutting to the site of Limecraigs sheds and sidings.

PLACES TO VISIT
● Mull of Kintyre Lighthouse
● Machrihanish Golf Club
● Wee Picture House, Campbeltown
● Campbeltown Museum & Heritage Centre

Right *Passengers from a Clyde steamer wait to board the 'Steamer Express' at the Hall Street terminus in Campbeltown, circa 1930. The Royal Hotel can be seen in the distance.*

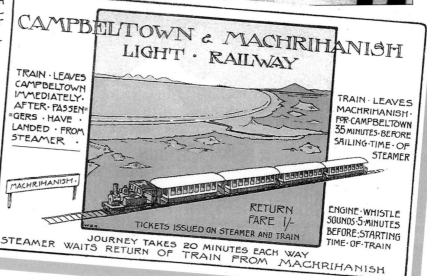

Above and right *Spot the differences on these two versions of the only official Campbeltown & Machrihanish Light Railway postcard issued. Daytrippers from Glasgow were only allowed 35 minutes to sample the delights of Machrihanish before making the return train journey to Campbeltown!*

ISLE OF MAN RAILWAYS

DOUGLAS TO PORT ERIN, PEEL AND RAMSEY

Located in the Irish Sea, midway between Scotland, England and Ireland, the Isle of Man is a self-governing Crown dependency and a member of the British Commonwealth. Inhabited since the Stone Age, the island and its fiercely independent people have a rich historical and cultural past. The Celts, early Christians, Vikings, Scots and English have all left their mark on this unique island and, today, their legacy sits comfortably alongside international banking and prosperity.

By the early 19th century, ferry services had started to operate from mainland England and the island, already patronised by Queen Victoria, became an increasingly popular destination for summer tourists. The regular ferry crossings from Liverpool also encouraged thousands of English workers and their families to spend their holidays here. In 1863, important electoral reforms introduced by the House of Keys were approved by the British Crown. This gave the Manx people more autonomy in spending locally raised revenue to improve transport, agriculture and education. Attracted by this stability, optimistic Victorian investors poured into the island, building hotels and railways.

HISTORY OF THE LINES

The mountainous nature of the island ruled out the construction of standard gauge lines so the railways of the Isle of Man were all built, apart from the electric Snaefell Mountain Railway, to a narrow gauge of 3ft. First registered in 1870, the Isle of Man Railway appointed Henry Vignoles as its engineer. The company put forward plans to construct lines from Douglas to Peel, with an extension from St John's to Ramsey, and from Douglas to Castletown. However, the extension to

Ramsey was dropped due to lack of support and the line to Castletown was extended to Port Erin, where the construction of a deep water harbour was planned.

Following the valleys of the Rivers Dhoo, Greba and Nebb across the centre of the island, the 11½-mile line from Douglas to Peel opened on 1 July 1873. Motive power was initially provided by three 2-4-0 tank locomotives supplied by Beyer Peacock of Manchester and these were named *Sutherland*, *Derby* and *Pender*. Two more similar locomotives, *Loch* and *Mona*, were delivered in 1874 prior to the opening of the 15½-mile steeply graded line to Port Erin on 1 August.

Although the Isle of Man Railway's decision not to go ahead with an extension from St John's

Above *No. 16 Mannin at Kirk Braddan station with an engineer's special in July 1963. The station was being smartened up prior to a visit by the Queen Mother.*

Left *In June 1961 a Beyer Peacock 2-4-0 tank locomotive trundles along the coastline near St Germains on the former Manx Northern Railway line to Ramsey.*

Below *Double-headed by 2-4-0 tank locomotives No.11* Maitland *and No.5* Mona, *a nine-coach train makes a vigorous start from Douglas with the 10.25am train for Ramsey in June 1961. The platform canopies have since been removed.*

to Ramsey was apparently taken due to lack of support, it wasn't long before the people of Ramsey were regretting being left out in the cold. Consequently, the Manx Northern Railway was formed to fill the gap and construction work started in March 1878. With the completion of viaducts across Glen Mooar and Glen Wyllin, the circuitous 16½-mile line opened

to traffic in September 1879. Motive power was initially provided by two 2-4-0 tank locomotives, named *Ramsey* and *Northern*, supplied by Sharp, Stewart of Manchester. A third locomotive, *Thornhill*, was supplied in 1880 by Beyer Peacock.

A third railway company, the Foxdale Railway Company, was registered in November 1882. The 2½-mile line from St John's to Foxdale was built primarily to serve lead mines near the latter village and the line was opened in August 1886. The Foxdale branch was operated from the outset by the Manx Northern Railway, who took over the line in 1891 when the original company went into liquidation. To cope with the extra traffic forecast to originate from the branch, the Manx Northern Railway

ordered a powerful 0-6-0 tank locomotive, named *Caledonia*, from Dübs of Glasgow. By 1911, the lead mines had closed and the infrequent passenger service was reduced to a locomotive and one coach.

The Manx Northern Railway was absorbed by the Isle of Man Railway in 1905, giving the enlarged company a total of 46 route miles. By this date four more 2-4-0 tank locomotives, named *Fenella, Douglas, G. H. Wood* and *Maitland,* had been delivered to the company by Beyer Peacock. A further three of these locomotives were delivered in 1908 (*Hutchinson*), 1910 (*Kissack*) and 1926 (*Mannin*).

The final railway to be built on the Isle of Man was a short branch line from Peel to Knockaloe. Opened in 1915 during World War I to serve an alien internment camp, the line was owned by the UK government but operated by the IoMR. Following the end of the war the line had lost its *raison d'etre* and was closed in 1920.

With increasing numbers of holidaymakers visiting the island from mainland Britain, the Isle of Man Railway initially went from strength to

Above *Despite total closure of the system in 1965, the Isle of Man Railway has come back to life on the Douglas to Port Erin line. Here, a train departs from Douglas behind a Beyer Peacock 2-4-0 in 2005.*

strength. Passenger numbers peaked in 1920 with over 1.6 million carried. However, with economic recession and increased competition from motor buses. this figure had dropped dramatically to just over 600,000 passengers by 1930. Despite the loss of holidaymakers during World War II, the railways were kept busy transporting service personnel and prisoners of war. The end of World War II brought an upsurge, with over 1.5 million passengers being carried in 1947. By now, however, the Isle of Man Railway, with its vintage locomotives and rolling stock and a backlog of track maintenance, was struggling to survive. By 1960, passenger numbers had dropped below the million mark and the writing was on the wall for the whole system. In that year, in an effort to reduce running costs, the IoMR purchased two diesel railcars from the defunct County Donegal Railway in Ireland.

The Foxdale branch had long ago lost its passenger service and, in an effort to curb further financial losses, all passenger services were withdrawn between St John's and Ramsey during the winter months from the Autumn of 1961. The rest of the system struggled on until November 1965, when it was abruptly closed down 'for urgent track maintenance'. Days, months and years dragged on and the IoMR remained closed. It looked like the end until the Marquess of Ailsa turned up and took over the Isle of Man Railway on a 21 year lease. However, trains would only run during the summer months.

Amidst great ceremony, Douglas to Peel trains

Left *A Port Erin to Douglas train departs from Castletown in September 2005. Passengers ride in beautifully restored Victorian carriages.*

recommenced running on 3 June 1967 and the St John's to Ramsey service on the next day. The Port Erin line reopened on 11 July, but trains ran only as far as Castletown. This stay of execution was short-lived, as the Douglas to Peel and St John's to Ramsey lines closed for good at the end of the 1968 summer season. The following year, the Douglas to Port Erin line reopened for the summer as the Isle of Man Victorian Steam Railway and, with financial aid from the Manx Government, the Marquess of Ailsa struggled on until 1971 when he relinquished his lease which reverted back to the Isle of Man Railway. With continuing subsidies from the Government, the Port Erin line struggled on during the summer months until 1978 when the Manx Government took the bold and farsighted decision to nationalise the little railway. A precedent for this had already been set in 1957 when the Manx

Above *No. 10 G. H. Wood halts at Ballasalla in July 1963 with the 2.15pm train from Douglas to Port Erin. Now over 100 years old, this locomotive is still in use on the Isle of Man Railway today*

Electric Railway (see p.152) from Douglas to Ramsey, via Laxey, was nationalised to save it from closure.

Today, the Isle of Man Railway comes under the auspices of the Department of Tourism and Transport and, with continued growth in passenger numbers, its future looks assured.

THE LINES TODAY

Douglas to Port Erin: The only remaining part of the Isle of Man Railway still operating, the Douglas to Port Erin line is now very much an important tourist attraction on the Isle of Man. It also provides an alternative form of transport for

Left *Waiting to take on water, No.11* Maitland *simmers outside Port Erin engine shed after hauling a train from Douglas in September 2005.*

locals wanting to shop in Douglas.

Major improvements have taken place, including relaying the majority of the line as part of the Department of Transport's IRIS sewerage scheme, and converting level crossings from manual to automatic operation.

The nine stations along the line – Douglas, Port Soderick, Santon, Balasalla, Castletown, Ballabeg, Colby, Port St Mary and Port Erin – have all been tastefully restored. The Steam Railway Museum at Port Erin, housed in a converted bus garage and old goods shed, has on display two locomotives (*Peveril* and *Mannin*), two royal carriages, memorabilia, photographs and relics going back to the opening of the island's first railways in 1873.

Today, motive power is provided by six of the original Beyer Peacock 2-4-0 tank locomotives, the oldest of which is 135-year-old *Loch*, and the unique 0-6-0 *Caledonia,* while passengers are carried in Victorian splendour in beautifully restored carriages. Services currently

operate between March and November, with trains taking a leisurely 57 minutes to complete the 15½ mile journey between Douglas and Port Erin.

For more details of the Isle of Man Railways, including timetables and fares, visit: www.visitisleofman.com

Douglas to Peel: Although the last train ran on 7 September 1968, the track on this section of the IoMR was not finally lifted until 1976. In the same year, the trackbed was purchased by the Manx Government and, in 1982, the section between Union Mills and Peel became a public footpath. Two years later the section from Quarter Bridge, on the western outskirts of Douglas, to Union Mills was also opened as a footpath. The 10-mile waymarked footpath is known as the Steam Heritage Trail and, at St John's, links up with footpaths to Sulby (15 miles) along the trackbed of the line to Ramsey and along the trackbed of the Foxdale branch (1 mile). During TT races the section between Quarter Bridge and Braddan doubles up as an access road for local residents. En route, the Heritage Trail passes under several road bridges, including those at Braddan and Union Mills. The platform and a railway hand crane mounted on a short stretch of track can be

Below *A train from Douglas approaches Port St Mary on the preserved Isle of Man Railway. The distant signal on the left warns the driver of the automated level crosssing that lies ahead. In the distance the village of Ballafesson nestles in the valley between the South Barrule hills and Bradda Head.*

Above *Although this photograph of Port Erin station was taken in April 1950, the scene today has not changed very much. No. 11 Maitland stands outside the engine shed after hauling a train from Douglas.*

Left *No. 11* Maitland *arrives at Crosby on the Douglas to Peel line with a children's picnic special to Kirk Michael on 29 June 1961. Closed in 1968, this section of railway forms part of the Steam Heritage Trail.*

seen at the latter station site. Further west, the crossing keepers huts at Crosby and Ballacraine now provide walkers with shelter during inclement weather. Since closure, the station building at Peel has been incorporated into a museum of island life known as the House of Manannan. *Note:* It has recently been announced that the Manx Department of Transport plan to install a main sewage pipe and associated pumping stations along the route between Peel and Union Mills. Although only one part of the Steam Heritage Trail will be closed at any one time, walkers and cyclists will face two years of disruption until the work is completed in 2010.

Foxdale Branch: The lead mines closed in 1911 and passenger services ceased in 1943. Although this branch from St John's then saw little use, the track was not lifted until 1974. The trackbed from Lower Foxdale is now a public footpath which links up with the Steam Heritage Trail at St John's, where the former Foxdale Railway station building is now a private residence. The former station building at Foxdale is now in use as a

Above *Built in 1874, Beyer Peacock 2-4-0 tank locomotive No 5* Mona *poses with driver, fireman and a visitor at St John's in June 1961. St John's was once a busy junction with lines radiating out to Douglas in the east, Peel in the west, Ramsey in the north and Foxdale in the south.*

Below *The Foxdale Branch was opened in 1886 to serve lead mines in the area. Nominally independent, the Foxdale Railway Company was taken over by the Manx Northern Railway in 1891. The lead mines closed in 1911 and the sparse passenger service ceased to run in 1943. This view of the little-used branch was taken near Foxdale in July 1933.*

MANX ELECTRIC RAILWAY

During the height of the Victorian tourist boom on the Isle of Man a unique and, at that time, technologically advanced electric railway was built northwards from Douglas following the beautiful and rugged coastline to the port of Ramsey. Opened in stages between 1893 and 1899, with a branch to the summit of the island's only mountain Snaefell (2.036ft above sea level), the line became an instant success with visitors. This scenic railway with its unique American-style trams was saved from closure in 1957 when it was nationalised by the Manx Government. With much of the rolling stock still in its original form a trip on this historic line is like a journey back in time.

Left *No. 12* Hutchinson *crosses Glen Mooar Viaduct with the 10.25am train from Douglas to Ramsey in July 1963. Today, only the ivy-clad masonry supports remain in what is now a Manx National Glen.*

community centre.

St John's to Ramsey: Branching off the Douglas to Peel line a short distance to the west of St John's, the 16½-mile former Manx Northern Railway route to Ramsey closed in September 1968 and the track was lifted in 1974. The trackbed from St Germain's to Bishopscourt, north of Kirk Michael, has since been incorporated into the 95-mile Raad ny Foillan long distance path around the coast of the Isle of Man.

Closely hugging the coast, the 8½-mile section of this footpath between St Germain's, where the former station building is now a private residence, and Bishopscourt takes in some of the most beautiful coastal scenerty on the island. The two major engineering works on this line were the viaducts across Glen Mooar and Glen Wyllin, just south of Kirk Michael. Although the girders have long been removed, the ivy-clad stone supports are still in place as a fitting tribute to this little railway. Both Glen Mooar and Glen Wyllin are owned by the Government and designated as Manx National Glens. Kirk Michael station, where there is a short length of track and a level crossing gate, is now a fire station. North of Kirk Michael, the Raad ny Foillan long distance path

Below *Only three months before closure, No. 12* Hutchinson *heads north along the coastline near Lady Port with a train for Ramsey. At this late stage, the trackbed was already being taken over by Nature!*

ORDNANCE SURVEY MAP
Landranger 1:50,000 series No. 95

HOW TO GET THERE
By air There are direct flights to Ronaldsay Airport from many airports in the UK and the Republic of Ireland.
By sea Car and passenger ferry services from Liverpool, Heysham, Belfast and Dublin are operated by the Isle of Man Steam Packet Company (tel. 08705 523 523).
Website: www.steam-packet.com

TOURIST INFORMATION
There are Tourist Information Centres in all of the main towns, at the airport and at Douglas Sea Terminal. For more details contact Isle of Man Tourist Information Centre (tel. 01624 686766) or visit: www.isleofman.com

WHERE TO STAY
There is a wide range of accommodation on The Isle of Man. For more details contact Isle of Man Tourist Information Centre (see above)

RAILWAY WALKS
Fortunately, the Manx Government had the wisdom to purchase the trackbed of the Douglas to Peel railway and about half of the St John's to Ramsey railway after track had been lifted in the 1970s. Passing through some of the most scenic parts of the island, both of these have since been converted into waymarked cycle and foot paths.
Douglas to Peel: The 10-mile waymarked footpath from Quarter Bridge, on the western outskirts of Douglas, to Peel is known as the Steam Heritage Trail and, at Peel links up with the Raad ny Foillan Long Distance Path along part of the trackbed of the line to Ramsey.
St Germain's to Kirk Michael: The trackbed from St Germain's to Bishopscourt, 1½ miles north of Kirk Michael, has since been incorporated into the 95-mile Raad ny Foillan Long Distance Path around the coast of the Isle of Man. Closely hugging the coast, the 8½-mile section of this footpath between St Germain's and Kirk Michael takes in some of the most beautiful coastal scenerty on the island. South of Kirk Michael, the ivy-clad stone supports for the former viaducts at Glen Mooar and Glen Wyllin are still in place as a fitting tribute to this little railway which closed in September 1968. Both Glen Mooar and Glen Wyllin are now designated as Manx National Glens.

PLACES TO VISIT
- Curraghs Wildlife Park
- Snaefell Mountain Railway
- Groudle Glen Railway
- Isle of Man Steam Railway
- Douglas Horse Tramway
- Laxey Wheel
- Tynwald Hill, St John's
- Peel Castle and Cathedral
- Castle Rushen
- Calf of Man bird sanctuary

leaves the railway trackbed to follow the coastline to Point of Ayre and then down to Ramsey.

Closely following the TT route along the A3, the trackbed of the railway now veers off to the east towards Ramsey. At Ballaugh the former goods shed has been restored, while the former crossing-keepers lodge near the Curraghs Wildlife Park is now a private residence. Apart from its wildlife, the park also has a passenger-carrying miniature railway which operates on weekends between April and October. Further east, Sulby Glen station is also a private residence, as are those at Sulby Bridge and Lezayre. Sadly the station building at Ramsey was demolished in 1978.

Left *No. 12* Hutchinson *crosses Glen Wyllin Viaduct with the 3.54pm train from Ramsey to Douglas in June 1968. Sadly, this scenic route of the Isle of Man Railway closed a few months later. Glen Wyllin has been designated a Manx National Glen.*

Right *No. 11* Maitland *passes over the level crossing at Ballaugh on 28 June 1961. This scene disappeared forever in September 1968.*

INDEX

BIBLIOGRAPHY

Narrow Gauge Locomotives; R W Kidner; The Oakwood Press 1939

Lost Lines: British Narrow Gauge; Nigel Welbourn; Ian Allan 2000

The English Narrow Gauge Railway; J D C A Prideaux;
    David & Charles 1978

The Glyn Valley Tramway; David Llewellyn Davies;
    The Oakwood Press 1966

The Ashover Light Railway; K P Plant; The Oakwood Press 1987

The Rye & Camber Tramway; Peter A Harding 1985

The Lynton & Barnstaple Railway 1895-1935; L T Catchpole;
    The Oakwood Press 2005

The Lynton & Barnstaple Railway; G A Brown, J D C A Prideaux,
    H G Ratcliffe; Surrey Support Group of the Lynton & Barnstaple
    Railway Trust 2006

The Ashover Light Railway; Robert Gratton and Stuart R Band;
    Wild Swan Publications 1989

The Narrow Gauge Railways of Wales 5th ed; R W Kidner;
    The Oakwood Press

Forgotten Railways; H P White; David St John Thomas/David & Charles
    1986

Narrow Gauge Album; P B Whitehouse; Ian Allan 1957

Branch Line to Southwold; Vic Mitchell and Keith Smith;
    Middleton Press 1984

The Last Days of the Old Corris; G Briwant-Jones; Gomer Press 2003

The Campbeltown & Machrihanish Light Railway; A D Farr;
    The Oakwood Press 1987

Great Western Corris; G Briwant-Jones; Gomer Press 2001

The Southwold Railway & Blyth Valley Walk; Southwold Railway Society

The Manifold Valley and its Light Railway; R Keys and L Porter;
    Moorland Publishing Co 1972

The Leek & Manifold Valley Light Railway; Keith Turner;
    Tempus Publishing 2005

The Leek & Manifold Valley Light Railway; Keith Turner;
    David & Charles 1980

The Welsh Highland Railway; John Stretton;
    Past & Present Publishing 1999

Douglas to Ramsey; Tom Heavyside; Middleton Press 2004

Douglas to Peel; Tom Heavyside; Middleton Press 2002

Douglas to Port Erin; Tom Heavyside; Middleton Press 2000

An Illustrated History of the Welsh Highland Railway; Peter Johnson;
    Oxford Publishing Co 2002

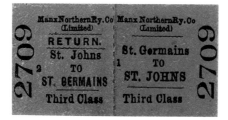

ACKNOWLEDGEMENTS

Design Julian Holland and Nigel White

Editing Denise Stobie

Picture research and commissioned photography Julian Holland

Photographic acknowledgements

t = top; b = bottom; r = right; l = left; m = middle

H. C. Casserley: contents pages; 9br; 26t; 28; 29b; 31; 33; 34b; 38b; 40; (58t; 67b Richard Casserley) 67t; 84; 85b; 87b; 88b; 90b; 92; 94t; 99b; 104t; 132; 136/137; 139t; 149t; 151b

Tony Harden: half-title page; 10b; 12b; 15t; 17t; 18b; 21t; 23t; 25tr; 27b; 43b; 44b; 48t; 50t; 53bl; 55b; 66bl;

68bl; 69br; 79t; 81t; 81b; 83tr; 105tr; 108; 110t; 111br; 112tl; 112b; 117br; 118t; 119t; 120bl; 123t; 124t; 126t; 127tr; 130tl; 134mr; 141mr; 141bl; 141br

Julian Holland: title page; 6/7; 8; 11; 13; 14; 16/17; 18t; 19; 20; 22; 24; 25tl; 25b; 26b; 30t; 32; 34t; 35; 36/37; 37t; 38/39; 39b; 41t; 42; 45; 46; 49; 50/51; 52; 53tr; 54; 55tl; 56; 57b; 58b; 59t; 59b; 60; 61b; 63; 64; 65; 68/69; 70; 73b; 74; 75t; 76t; 77; 78; 80; 82; 86; 86tr; 89; 91; 93b; 95; 96/97; 97tr; 98; 100; 102t; 103; 105b; 106t; 107; 109t; 111; 113b; 114; 115tl; 115br; 116; 119b;

120/121t; 121bl; 121r; 122; 125; 127; 128; 129tl; 129r; 130b; 131bl; 131br; 133br; 134bl; 134/135t; 135br; 138tl; 138/139b; 140t; 145t; 146; 148tl; 148/149b; 159

Ivo Peters Collection: 12t; 142; 143br; 144; 147t; 150; 151tr; 152; 153b; 154; 155br

Rail Archive Stephenson: 72; 79br

Transport Treasury: 15b (Dr Ian C Allen); 47t (Dr Ian C Allen); 71br